MW01298358

CELEBRATING THE BIRTH OF THE PROPHET ﷺ

Imperial celebration of the *Mawlid al-Nabi al-Sharif* or Blessed Birth of the Prophet ﷺ in the Sultan Ahmed (Blue) Mosque, Istanbul, in the presence of Sultan Mahmud II and Ottoman grandees. Source: D'Ohsson, *Tableau général de l'Empire othoman*, vol. I, after p. 256.

حَوْلَ الْإِحْتِفَالِ بِذِكْرى الْمَوْلِدِ النَّبَوِيّ الشَّرِيفِ

CELEBRATING
the
BIRTH
of the
PROPHET

By the Muhaddith of Hijaz & Scion of the Prophetic House
MUHAMMAD B. 'ALAWI AL-MALIKI AL-HASANI

Translation & Notes
RASHAD JAMEER

Imam Ghazali
INSTITUTE

Title: CELEBRATING THE BIRTH OF THE PROPHET ﷺ
ISBN: 978-1-952306-06-8

SECOND EDITION

Author: MUHAMMAD B. ʿALAWI AL-MALIKI AL-HASANI
Translator: RASHAD JAMEER
Proofreaders: DR BANO MURTUJA | MOOSAA KHAN
Typeset: THE NOBLE ARK

REVIVAL PRESS
info@revivalpress.com

CONTENTS

FOREWORD

In the name of Allah, Most Gracious, Most Merciful

ALL PRAISE IS DUE TO ALLAH, and prayers and peace be upon our Master, the Messenger of Allah ﷺ Muhammad b. Abdullah, and upon his family and his Companions and those after him. To proceed:

Among the marvels of Allah Most High's handiwork is the affair of His selecting and electing His creation, and truly the greatest creation that Allah, the Exalted and Sublime, elected and filled with His munificence and generosity is our Master Muhammad ﷺ.

For this reason, orators and writers have used multifarious methods to describe him and discuss topics that continue to draw inspiration and 'drink' from the spring of mercy that Allah the Exalted and Sublime has gifted to us. May Allah have mercy on the one who said:

And his descriptors employ various methods to describe him
But time itself shall come to an end, yet there shall
remain about him what is yet to be described".

In reality, people are discussing the gift of Allah that will never diminish and the power of Allah that will never be incapacitated, regarding that which was granted to the greatest of creation, our Master Muhammad ﷺ. Truly among what has become well-known among the people of the Prophetic Way and the majority (*ahl al-sunnah wa al-jama'ah*) is the love of commemorating and celebrating his ﷺ mention; as a proclamation of their allegiance and love, as a means (*wasila*) of emulating his Sunnah and guidance, in

9

seeking to revive his life in their hearts and in their states, as a tie to the followers of the greatest one ever followed (*al-matbu al-azam*)ﷺ and to enrich the connection between the Umma and its Prophet ﷺ.

Al-'Allama, the Sayyid, Muhammad b. 'Alawi al-Maliki al-Hasani al-Makki advocated, in several of his writings, that these objectives and actions indicate to its being recommended via the Book, the sayings of the leader of the beloveds (*sayyid al-ahbab*), the guidance of the Pious Forebearers from the Companions, the Followers, and the Imams who acted upon their knowledge, the sages, the righteous, and the elect of the Umma. Among these writings is his fine letter entitled '*Celebrating the Birth of the Prophet* ﷺ' which, due to its importance, has been published several times over, indicative of the need for what is found therein.

From among the outward signs of goodness that Allah, the Exalted and Sublime, has manifested is the translation of '*Celebrating the Birth of the Prophet* ﷺ' by our brother Rashad b. Sulayman, who undertook the task of translating it into the English language; hoping for benefit and to spread goodness and excellent manners in the way of the elite Imams, in elucidating what the Umma needs of elucidation with the proofs of *ahl al-sunnah wa al-jama'ah* in what they delve in and what they are concerned with.

May Allah show Imam Malik mercy for his statement, "It is not Sunnah to argue about the Sunnah. Rather, one should convey the Sunnah if it will be accepted, otherwise he should remain silent". Celebrating the Prophet's noble birth is from the derived Sunnahs which are subsumed under the Shariah's general principles and its actions are founded upon the Lord's address to His servants and the guidance of the Chosen One (*al-mustafa*) ﷺ which he left behind for his Umma.

May Allah reward with goodness anyone who partakes in reviving the connections between the Umma and between its Prophet and connects the generations with their past and especially with the guidance of their Prophet ﷺ. We ask Allah, Exalted and Sublime is He, to place blessings in this translation and those who facilitated it, and to provide us and him with truthfulness and sincerity in benefitting the Umma and to make our actions, in their entirety, in accordance to our Master Muhammad ﷺ, and to provide us on the Day of Judgment with his goodly company ﷺ in well-being.

May Allah send blessings and peace upon our Master Muhammad, and upon his folk and his Companions. Amin.

UMAR B. HUSAYN B. UMAR AL-KHATIB AL-ANSARI
Dar al-Mustafa Centre for the Islamic Sciences
16 SAFAR 1437 AH | 29 NOVEMBER 2015 CE

PUBLISHER'S MESSAGE

In the name of Allah, Most Gracious, Most Merciful

THROUGHOUT ONE'S LIFE there are many occasions of happiness that necessitate a celebration. Marriage, the birth of a child, the acquisition of a new job etc., are all examples of moments where one may celebrate. In each of these instances, we celebrate according to the rank of these joyous occasions. When we speak about the birth of the greatest of creation ﷺ, we are speaking about the most momentous of occasions. Our teachers have taught us that the birth of the Prophet ﷺ (*mawlid*) calls for the highest levels and display of happiness.

The celebration of the birth of the Prophet ﷺ is a celebration of a man who is multi-faceted. He is an individual who inspired the rise of a civilization that, in many respects, enlightened the world in a period of darkness. His ﷺ teachings inspire young and old, and remain a beacon of hope in turbulent times.

In an age where celebrating the Mawlid has come under attack, we have found it necessary to provide a clear and concise text on celebrating the birth of the Prophet ﷺ. Sayyid Muhammad b. 'Alawi al-Maliki's text does precisely that. The late scholar's work on the issue of the Mawlid is one that is comprehensive, yet remains short and to the point. It is an easy read for an individual who wishes to have a solid understanding and foundation on the topic.

We ask Allah to accept our efforts, and allow us to continue to be servants of those who seek.

MUHAMMAD ADNAAN SATTAUR
Imam Ghazali Institute

TRANSLATOR'S INTRODUCTION

*In the Name of Allah, the Most Gracious, Most Merciful.
May peace, blessings and rest be upon our master
Muhammad, the ummi Prophet for the end of time, and
upon his Family, his Companions, and all those who
follow his way until Judgment Day.*

TO PROCEED: many Muslims worldwide have grown up celebrating
the birth of the Prophet 鬃 otherwise known as the Mawlid[1] or
Milad-e-Nabi. Historically the Mawlid has reached many Muslim
countries via the Yemeni Ba-Alawi clan. Countries such as India,
Singapore, Guyana, Malaysia, Indonesia, Egypt, Palestine, Turkey,
China, Russia, and Sudan and many more, all boast of a long-
standing tradition of holding gatherings to celebrate the life and
times of the last Prophet of God, *Muhammad ur-Rasulullah salla
Allahu alayhi wa sallam.*

One should not be fooled into thinking that this was something
adopted, supported and endorsed by the uneducated commoners.
Rather, we find across hundreds of years, scholars of the greatest
calibre attending and even composing their own *Mawalid* along
with the pious. Do eminent scholars like Ibn Kathir and Ibn Hajar
al-Haytami, authors of respective Mawalid, compose literature for,
and attend gatherings that, promote anti-Islamic sentiments and
which oppose the Sacred Law? Are they to be considered innovators
in Islam?

Alhamdulilah, in our blessed city of Toronto, we have a renewal
of the Mawlid gathering, well-attended by the scholars and friends of

---

[1] The term Mawlid is used interchangeably to refer to the birth of the Prophet 鬃,
celebrations of the birth and the poems written in celebration of the birth.

Allah (*al-awliya*) from across the Muslim world. I found many people with genuine questions about one aspect of the Mawlid or another.

In an attempt to be a means (*wasila*) of spreading knowledge among Sufi circles or those attending gatherings of *dhikr*, Wasila Media has chosen to translate this slim, but potent, book by one of the greatest traditional scholars of this generation, Sayyid Muhammad al-'Alawi al-Maliki al-Hasani ﷺ.

Western society has become bent on trivializing and marginalizing anything connected to life after death, religion and the unseen world. This influence has, unfortunately, also crept into the Umma with the proliferation of the politically-sponsored ideology of Wahhabism. Wahhabism is characterized by an absurd and narrow-minded literalism (which stems from, ironically enough, nescience of the Arabic language) and not being trained and licensed by scholars who are part of an unbroken chain of masters going back to our collective master, Sayyiduna Muhammad ﷺ. As scholars explain, in the verse of the Qur'an which describes Sayyiduna Rasulillah ﷺ, ❨*calling to Allah by 'His permission'...*❩ (Qur'an 33:46). 'His permission' here includes training (*tarbiya*) at the hands of prophetic inheritors.

By disconnecting the Umma, not necessarily from the letter of the law of Allah and His Messenger, but from love of Allah and His Messenger ﷺ, the deadly physical and spiritual (*ruhani*) effects of the '*Qur'an and Sunnah Only*' movement have known no bounds.

The translation of this particular book, written in the Hijaz with this in mind, is a befitting work for the true seeker of knowledge. May Allah grant us the fear of Allah to implement the Shariah and grant us perfect love in loving and sacrificing for the Messenger of Allah and his inheritors. *Amin.*

★ ★ ★

I WOULD LIKE TO THANK Ustadh Siddique for his support and Muhammad Adnaan Sattaur and the IMAM GHAZALI INSTITUTE for bringing this work to fruition. I would like to thank the marifah. net team for the use of Shaykh Fakruddin al-Owaisi al-Madani's biography of Sayyid Muhammad al-ʿAlawi. Thanks also to Ahmad b. Aqil al-Hadrami. I was blessed to attend my first Mawlid in Cairo in 2008, at his *majlis*, which was a beautiful model of *dhikr* and *sunnah*; to al-Habib ʿUmar b. Hafiz and the team at DAR AL-MUSTAFA for the beautiful *mawalid* every Thursday, year-round, in Hadramawt and to all the *mawalid* in our *mubarak* city of Toronto. May Allah bless and accept, and increase our love and following of the Messenger of Allah ﷺ.

RAHSHAD JAMEER
23 SHAWWAL 1436 AH | 9 AUGUST 2015 CE
Toronto, CANADA

SAYYID MUHAMMAD B. 'ALAWI
AL-MALIKI AL-HASANI

INTRODUCTION

Sayyid Muhammad b. 'Alawi b. 'Abbas b. 'Abdul 'Aziz al-Maliki al-Hasani was one of the foremost traditional Islamic scholars of contemporary times, and without doubt, the most highly respected and loved scholar of the holy city of Mecca and the entire Hijaz region (Western Arabia). He is a grandson of the Prophet 鷗, a leader of the *ahl al-bayt*, the Imam of Hadith in our age, an authority of the four Madhhabs, a spiritual leader of the highest calibre, a caller to Allah *par excellence*, and unparalleled in his standing in the world of traditional Islamic scholarship. Visiting him was considered imperative for the Ulama who would visit Mecca.

FAMILY

The Sayyid descends from a noble family that is directly connected to the blessed Prophet Muhammad 鷗. He is a scion of the famous al-Maliki al-Hasani family of Mecca, who are descendants of the Prophet 鷗 through his grandson, Imam al-Hasan b. 'Ali 鷗.

The Maliki family is one of the most respected families in Mecca and has produced great scholars who taught in the Haram of Mecca for centuries. In fact, five of the Sayyid's ancestors have been the Maliki Imams of the Haram of Mecca. His grandfather, Sayyid 'Abbas al-Maliki, was the Mufti and Qadi of Mecca and the Imam and Khatib of the Haram. He held this position during the Ottoman, then Hashemite times, and continued to hold it after the Saudi Kingdom was established. The late King 'Abdul Aziz b. Saud had great respect for him.

His late father, Sayyid 'Alawi al-Maliki was one of the greatest Ulama of Mecca in the previous century. He taught the various traditional Islamic sciences in the Haram of Mecca for nearly 40 years. Hundreds of students from all over the Islamic world benefited from his lessons in the Haram and many hold key religious positions in their lands today. The late King Faisal would not make any decision regarding Mecca without consulting Sayyid 'Alawi. He passed away in 1971 and his funeral was the biggest funeral seen in Mecca in a 100 years. For three days after his death, the local Saudi radio stations only played the holy Qur'an. This was something that was only done for him.

The Maliki family has produced many other scholars, but for the sake of brevity we have only mentioned Sayyid Muhammad's eminent father and grandfather.

BIRTH AND EARLY EDUCATION

Sayyid Muhammad was born in 1946 in the holy city of Mecca. He was fortunate to have as his father the most learned scholar of Mecca, Sayyid 'Alawi al-Maliki. His father was his first and primary teacher, teaching him privately at home as well as at the Haram of Mecca, where he memorized the Holy Qur'an at a young age. He was educated by his father from childhood and was authorized to teach every book he studied with him.

FURTHER EDUCATION

Following his father's instruction, he studied and mastered various traditional Islamic sciences including Aqidah, Tafsir, Hadith, Fiqh, Usul, Mustalah and Nahw, at the feet of other great scholars of Mecca, as well as Medina, all of whom granted him full certification (*ijazah*) to teach these sciences to others. By the age of 15, the Sayyid was already teaching books of Hadith and Fiqh in the Haram of Mecca to fellow students, by the orders of his teachers.

After finishing his traditional education in his hometown of Mecca, he was sent by his father to study at the esteemed al-Azhar University of Egypt. He received his Ph.D from al-Azhar at the age of 25, making him the first and youngest Saudi to earn a Ph.D from there. His thesis on Hadith was rated 'excellent,' and highly praised by the eminent Ulama of al-Azhar at that time, such as Imam Abu Zahra ☙.

TRAVELS IN QUEST OF KNOWLEDGE

It has been the way of most great Ulama to travel in pursuit of knowledge and wisdom. The Sayyid was no exception to this rule. He traveled from a young age, with the permission of his father, to seek knowledge and spirituality from those who possess it. He traveled extensively in North Africa, Egypt, Sudan, Syria, Turkey, and the Indo-Pak subcontinent to learn from great scholars, meet the Friends of Allah, visit the Mosques and Shrines, and collect manuscripts and books. In each of these lands, he met its great Ulama and Awliya and benefited immensely from them. They, in turn, were also very impressed by this young student from Mecca and gave him special attention. Many had great respect for his learned father already, so were extremely honored to have the son as their student.

LICENSES TO TRANSMIST (*ijazat*)

The traditional system of Islamic education is based on the permission to transmit Sacred Knowledge (*ijazah*). Not just any person is allowed to teach; only those who have certified *ijazat* from well-known scholars. For every branch of knowledge and for every book of Hadith, Fiqh, Tafsir there are chains of narration (*isnad*) that go back to the author of the book himself through his students and their students; and, in the case of most isnad, such as those of the Qur'an, Hadith and Tasawwuf, they connect back to the blessed Prophet ﷺ.

Sayyid Muhammad was honored to be a Shaykh with one of the largest number of *ijazat* in our times. He also possessed the closest, i.e. shortest, chains of narration, to his ancestor, the Prophet Muhammad ﷺ. In his Arabian homeland and in the course of his travels, the Sayyid obtained more than 200 *ijazat* from the greatest scholars of his time, in every branch of Islamic knowledge. Thus, his own *ijazah*, that he would grant to his students, was from the most prestigious and rarest in the world, linking his students to countless great scholars.

Indeed, most of the great Scholars today had sought *ijazah* from the Sayyid. The Masters who granted the Sayyid their respective *ijazat* were great savants and shining stars from all over the Islamic world. I would like to mention a few here:

FROM MECCA AL-MUKARRAMA
- His learned father and first teacher,
  Sayyid 'Alawi b. 'Abbas al-Maliki
- Shaykh Muhammad Yahya Aman al-Makki
- Shaykh al-Sayyid Muhammad al-Arabi al-Tabbani
- Shaykh Hasan Said al-Yamani
- Shaykh Hasan b. Muhammad al-Mashshat
- Shaykh Muhammad Nur Sayf
- Shaykh Muhammad Yasin al-Fadani
- Al-Sayyid Muhammad Amin Kutbi
- Al-Sayyid Ishaq b. Hashim Azuz
- Al-Habib Hasan b. Muhammad Fad'aq
- Al-Habib Abdul Qadir b. Aydarus al-Bar
- Shaykh Khalil Abd-al-Qadir Taybah
- Shaykh Abd-Allah Sa'id al-Lahji

FROM MEDINA AL-MUNAWWARA
- Shaykh Hasan al-Sha'ir, Shaykh al-Qurra of Medina
- Shaykh Diya'uddin Ahmad al-Qadiri
- Al-Sayyid Ahmad Yasin al-Khiyari
- Shaykh Muhammad al-Mustafa al-Alawi al-Shinqiti

- Shaykh Ibrahim al-Khatani al-Bukhari
- Shaykh Abdul Ghafur al-Abbasi al-Naqshbandi

FROM HADRAMAWT AND YEMEN
- Al-Habib Umar b. Ahmad b. Sumayt,
  Grand Imam of Hadramawt
- Shaykh al-Sayyid Muhammad Zabarah, Mufti of Yemen
- Shaykh al-Sayyid Ibrahim b. Aqil al-Ba-Alawi, Mufti of Ta'iz
- Al-Imam al-Sayyid Ali b. Abdul Rahman al-Hibshi
- Al-Habib Alawi ibn Abdullah b. Shihab
- Al-Sayyid Hasan b. Abdul Bari al-Ahdal
- Shaykh Fadhl b. Muhammad Ba-Fadhal
- Al-Habib Abdullah b. Alawi al-Attas
- Al-Habib Muhammad b. Salim b. Hafeez
- Al-Habib Ahmad Mashhur al-Haddad
- Al-Habib Abdul Qadir al-Saqqaf
- Shaykh Abdullah Zayd al-Zabidi

FROM SYRIA AND LEBANON
- Shaykh Abul Yusr ibn Abidin, Mufti of Syria
- Shaykh al-Sayyid al-Sharif Muhammad al-Makki al-Kattani,
  Mufti of the Malikis
- Shaykh Muhammad Asad al-Abaji, Mufti of the Shafi'i
- Shaykh al-Sayyid Muhammad Salih al-Farfur
- Shaykh Hasan Habannakah al-Maydani
- Shaykh Abdul Aziz Uyun al-Sud al-Himsi
- Shaykh Muhammad Said al-Idlabi al-Rifai
- Shaykh Abdullah al-Harari

FROM EGYPT
- Shaykh al-Sayyid Muhammad al-Hafiz al-Tijani,
  Imam of Hadith in Egypt
- Shaykh Hasanayn Muhammad Makhluf, Mufti of Egypt
- Shaykh Salih al-Jafari, Imam of al-Azhar
- Shaykh Amin Mahmud Khattab al-Subki
- Shaykh Muhammad al-Aquri (student of Imam al-Bajuri)

- Shaykh Hasan al-Adawi
- Shaykh al-Sayyid Muhammad Abul Uyun al-Khalwati
- Al-Imam al-Akbar Dr.Abdul Halim Mahmud,
  Rector of al-Azhar

FROM NORTH AFRICA (MOROCCO, ALGERIA, LIBYA AND TUNISIA)
- Al-Sharif Idris al-Sanusi, late King of Libya
- Shaykh al-Sayyid Abdullah b. al-Siddiq al-Ghumari,
  Imam of Hadith in Morocco
- Shaykh al-Sayyid Abdul Aziz b. al-Siddiq al-Ghumari
- Shaykh Muhammad al-Tahir ibn Ashur,
  Imam of al-Zaytuna, Tunis
- Shaykh al-Sayyid al-Sharif Abdul Kabir al-Saqali al-Mahi
- Shaykh al-Tayyib al-Muhaji al-Jaza'iri, Muhaddith of Algeria
- Shaykh al-Faruqi al-Rahhali al-Marrakashi
- Shaykh al-Sayyid al-Sharif Muhammad al-Muntasir al-Kattani
- Shaykh Sidi Muhammad Bal-Qa'id al-Hibri
  al-Shadhili al-Darqawi

FROM THE INDO-PAK SUBCONTINENT
- Shaykh al-Faqih Abul Wafa al-Afghani,
  Imam of the Hanafis, Hyderabad Deccan
- Shaykh al-Allamah Abdul Muid Khan, Hyderabad Deccan
- al-Imam al-Arif-Billah Mustafa Rida Khan al-Barelawi,
  Mufti of India
- Mufti Muhammad Shafii al-Deobandi, Mufti of Pakistan
- Mawlana Muhammad Zakariyyah al-Kandahlawi,
  Master of Hadith
- Malawana Zafar Ahmad Thanawi, author of 'Ila al-Sunan
- Shaykh al-Muhaddith Habib al-Rahman al-Azami
- Mawlana Sayyid Abul Hasan Ali al-Nadawi

FROM THE SUDAN
- Shaykh Yusuf Hamad al-Nil
- Shaykh Majdhub Muddassir Ibrahim al-Tijani
- Shaykh Ibrahim Abul Nur
- Shaykh al-Tayyib Abu Qinayah al-Tijani

These were only the most famous of the scholars from whom he got *ijazat*, and there are many others. In Sayyid Muhammad al-Maliki, we find the best of all these Shayukh from various backgrounds and inclinations. The Sayyid's broadmindedness in his quest for knowledge is an example for all those who wish to restrict themselves to one school or institute.

HIS TEACHING CAREER

One would not like to use the word 'career' for the Sayyid's teaching activities, as it seems closely connected to material gains. The Sayyid however, like all traditional Shayukh, and like his ancestors before him, taught solely for the sake of Allah; and neither expected or gained any material benefit. In fact, he would host a large number of students at his own residence, providing them with food, drink, shelter, clothes, books and everything else they needed. In return, they were only required to follow the rules and etiquette of students of sacred knowledge. These students would usually stay with him for many years, learning the various branches of Islamic knowledge, then return to their lands. Hundreds of students learnt at his feet and have become savants of Islamic knowledge and spirituality in their countries, particularly Indonesia, Malaysia, Egypt, Yemen and Dubai.

After returning from al-Azhar, he was appointed as Professor of Islamic Studies at the Umm al-Qura University in Mecca, where he taught from 1970. In 1971, after his father's death, the scholars of Mecca asked him to accept his father's position as a teacher in the Haram, which he did. Thus, he sat on the chair from which his family had taught for more than a century. He also occasionally taught in the Haram of Medina. His lessons were the largest attended lessons in the Two Harams.

In the early eighties, he was relinquished of both his teaching position in the Umm al-Qura University as well as his ancestral chair of teaching in the Haram, due to the edicts (fatwas) of some fanatical scholars of the Wahhabi sect, who considered his presence a threat to their extremist ideology and religious authority.

Since then, he taught the great books of Hadith, Fiqh, Tafsir and Tasawwuf at his home and mosque on al-Maliki Street in the Rusayfah district of Mecca; and his public lessons, between Maghrib and Isha, were attended by no less than 500 people daily. Many students from the University would attend his lessons in the evenings. Despite opposition from the Wahhabi establishment, Sayyid Muhammad al-Maliki was highly respected by the Saudi government and was often consulted by the King on important affairs. He was also nominated as the head judge at the international Qira'at (Qur'anic reading) competition in Mecca for three consecutive years.

HIS WRITINGS

He was a prolific writer and produced close to one hundred works. He has written on a variety of religious, legal, social and historical topics and many of his books are considered masterpieces on the subject and are prescribed textbooks in Islamic institutes around the world. We mention here some selected works on various subjects:

AQIDAH
- *Mafahim Yajib an Tusahhah*
- *Manhaj al-Salaf fi Fahm al-Nusus*
- *Al-Tahzir min al-Takfir*
- *Huwa Allah*
- *Qul Hadhihi Sabili*
- *Sharh Aqidat al-Awwam*

TAFSIR
- *Zubdat al-Itqan fi Ulum al-Qur'an*
- *Wa-Hiwa bil Ufuq al-Ala*
- *Al-Qawaid al-Asasiyya fi Ulum al-Qur'an*
- *Hawl Khasa'is al-Qur'an*

HADITH
- *Al-Manhal al-Latif fi Usul al-Hadith al-Sharif*
- *Al-Qawaid al-Asasiyya fi Ilm Mustalah al-Hadith*
- *Fadl al-Muwatta wa-Inayat al-Umma al-Islamiyya bihi*
- *Anwar al-Masalik fi al-Muqaranat bayna Riwayat al-Muwatta lil-Imam Malik*

SIRAH

- *Muhammad: al-Insan al-Kamil*
- *Tarikh al-Hawadith wal-Ahwal al-Nabawiyya*
- *'Urf al-Ta'arif bil-Mawlid al-Sharif*
- *Al-Anwar al-Bahiyya fi Isra' wal-Miraj Khayr al-Bariyya*
- *Al-Zakha'ir al-Muhammadiyya*
- *Zikriyat wa-Munasabat*
- *Al-Bushra fi Manaqib al-Sayyidat Khadijah al-Kubra*

USUL

- *Al-Qawaid al-Asasiyya fi Usul al-Fiqh*
- *Sharh Manzumat al-Waraqat fi Usul al-Fiqh*
- *Mafhum al-Tatawwur wa al-Tajdid fil Shariah al-Islamiyya*

FIQH

- *Al-Risalat al-Islamiyya Kamaluha wa-Khuluduha wa-Alamiyyatuha*
- *Labbayk Allahumma Labbayk*
- *Al-Ziyarat al-Nabawiyya bayn al-Sharia wa-al-Bidiyya*
- *Shifa' al-Fu'ad bi-Ziyarat Khayr al-Ibad*
- *Hawl al-Ihtifal bi-Zikra al-Mawlid al-Nabawi al-Sharif*
- *Al-Madh al-Nabawi bayn al-Ghuluww wal-Ijhaf*

TASAWWUF

- *Al-Mukhtar min Kalam al-Akhyar*
- *Abwab al-Faraj*
- *Shawariq al-Anwar min Adiyat al-Sadah al-Akhyar*
- *Al-Husun al-Maniyya*
- *Mukhtasar Shawariq al-Anwar*
- *Azkar Nabawiyya wa-Adiyyat Salafiyya*

MISCELLANEOUS

- *Fi Rihab al-Bayt al-Haram* (History of Mecca)
- *Al-Mustashriqun Bayn al-Insaf wa al-Asabiyya* (Study of Orientalism)
- *Nazrat al-Islam ila al-Riyada* (Sports in Islam)
- *Al-Qudwat al-Hasana fi Manhaj al-Da'wah ila Allah* (Methods of Dawah)

- *Ma La Aynun Ra'at*
  (Description of Paradise)
- *Nizam al-Usra fi al-Islam*
  (Islam and Family)
- *Kashf al-Ghumma*
  (Virtues of helping fellow Muslims)
- *Al-Dawat al-Islahiyya*
  (Call for Reform)
- *Al-Muslimun bayn al-Waqi' wa al-Tajriba*
  (Contemporary Muslim world)
- *Fi Sabil al-Huda wal-Rashad*
  (Collection of speeches)
- *Sharaf al-Ummat al-Islamiyya*
  (Superiority of the Muslim Umma)
- *Usul al-Tarbiyyat al-Nabawiyya*
  (Prophetic methods of education)
- *Nur al-Nibras fi Asanid al-Jadd al-Sayyid Abbas*
  (Set of Grandfather's Ijazat)
- *Al-Uqud al-Lu'liyya fil Asanid al-Alawiyya*
  (Set of father's Ijazat)
- *Al-Tali al-Said al-Muntakhab min al-Musalsalat wal Asanid*
  (Set of Ijazat)
- *Al-Iqd al-Farid al-Mukhtasar min al-Athbat wa al-Asanid*
  (Set of Ijazat)

There are many other publications that are not mentioned and many works that are yet to be published. We also did not list the numerous important classical works that the Sayyid located, researched and published for the first time, with notes and commentary. All together, the Sayyid's contribution has been great. Many of the Sayyid's works have also been translated into multiple languages.

He was a keen propagator of true Islamic guidance and spirituality and traveled all over Asia, Africa, Europe and America calling people to heed the Words of Allah and His final Messenger Muhammad ﷺ. In South-East Asia especially, the Sayyid personally established and ran more than 70 Islamic schools to counter Christian missionary activities. Large numbers of Christians and Buddhists embraced Islam at his blessed hands, many of them simply by looking at the Muhammadan Light shining on his face. Wherever he would go, the leaders, scholars and masses of that country would receive him with jubilation. He often addressed crowds of hundreds, and even thousands, of people. He was dearly loved and adored all over the Muslim world, not only because of his Muhammadan Lineage but also because of his immense knowledge, wisdom, humble manners and spiritual charisma. He was known to be extremely generous with his knowledge, wealth and time.

THE SAYYID'S 'APPROACH'

He followed and advocated the mainstream majority tradition of Islam, the way of *Ahl al-Sunnah wa al-Jama'ah*, the hallmark of which is tolerance and moderation, knowledge and spirituality, and unity in diversity. He believed in adherence to the four established Madhahib, but without fanaticism. He taught respect for the great Ulama and Awliya of the past.

He was against the hasty condemnation of fellow Muslims as disbelievers (*kufar*) and polytheists (*mushrikun*), something that has become the trademark of certain modern sects today. He was very critical of so-called 20th century 'reformers' who wish to simply wash away the Islam of previous generations in the name of 'pure Islam'. He believed that condemning all Ashari, Hanafi, Shafi'i, Maliki followers or all Sufis, as some extremist sects are doing nowadays, means condemning the whole Umma of Islam for the past thousand years. This can only be the attitude and approach of an enemy of Islam, not a friend.

The Sayyid strongly believed that the great Madhhab-following Sunni-Sufi Islamic scholars of the past thousand years are our connection to the Qur'an and Sunnah, and not a barrier between them and us, as some would like to believe. True understanding of the Qur'an and Sunnah is one that is based on the interpretation of the great scholars of Islam, not the whims and fancies of modern-day extremists who do not think twice before condemning the majority of the Muslims of the world. The Sayyid believed that the majority of this Umma are on the correct path, it's the fanatical minority groups that must recheck their extremist ideologies.

The Sayyid was also a proponent of true Shariah based Sufism, the Sufism of the great Awliya and saints of this Umma. He himself was a spiritual master of the highest caliber, linked to most of the great Spiritual Orders of Islam, through great Shayukh of the *Turuq* or spiritual orders. He believed that reciting *dhikr*, alone and in congregation, is an integral part of a Muslim's spiritual well-being. All his students were required to perform the night-vigil prayer (*tahajjud*) and read morning and evening litanies (*awrad*).

Finally, the Sayyid believed that Muslims must use their resources to uplift the state of the Umma, spiritually, socially and materially, and not waste their precious time in fighting over petty issues. He believed Muslims should not condemn each other on matters that have been differed upon by the Ulama, rather, they must join hands in combating that which is agreed upon to be evil and sinful.

The Sayyid's views are exemplified in his most famous work *Mafahim Yajib an Tusahhah* ('Concepts that should be rectified'), a book that gained wide appreciation throughout the Islamic world, and was highly acclaimed in scholarly circles.

HIS PASSING

He passed away on Friday, 15th of Ramadan 1426 / 29th October 2004 in a state of fasting in his house in Mecca. He had wished to pass away in Ramadan. The day after his passing, King Abdullah of

Saudi Arabia and all the top officials of the country and members of the Saudi royal family came to pay their condolences.

The Sayyid left behind two sons, Sayyid Ahmad and Sayyid Abdullah, and many daughters. Sayyid Ahmad is a learned young scholar and has become his father's able successor. He continues the teaching and spiritual activities of his father. The Sayyid also left behind a large number of students, many of whom hold prominent positions in Saudi Arabia and throughout the Muslim world. Through them, and through his works, his legacy continues to flourish.

May Allah grant him the highest place in Jannah next to his beloved Grandfather, Sayyidina Rasulillah ﷺ. *Amin.*

محمد صلى الله عليه وسلم

حَوْلُ الْاِحْتِفَالِ بِذِكْرَى الْمَوْلِدِ النَّبَوِيّ الشَّرِيفِ

CELEBRATING
the
BIRTH
of the
PROPHET

By the Muhaddith of Hijaz & Scion of the Prophetic House
MUHAMMAD B. ʿALAWI AL-MALIKI AL-HASANI

Translation & Notes
RASHAD JAMEER

Imam Ghazali
INSTITUTE

I
AUTHOR'S INTRODUCTION

*In the name of Allah, Most Gracious, Most Merciful,
Praise be to Allah, Lord of the worlds, and may
blessings and peace be upon the noblest of the Prophets
and Messengers, our Master Muhammad ﷺ, upon
his family, and all his Companions. To proceed:*

THERE HAS BEEN AMPLE DISCUSSION on the ruling of celebrating
the birth of the Prophet ﷺ. I was not planning to write on this
topic because what occupies my mind and the minds of the
Muslim intellectuals today is greater than this secondary issue. The
discussion about this issue happens annually, is read about every
Mawlid season, and circulated every year until people get tired of
hearing about it. However, when many of the brothers desired to
know my opinion, especially on this subject, and out of fear that
not responding will be deemed as concealing knowledge, I have
endeavoured to take part in writing on this topic, asking The Master
ﷻ that He inspire one and all with the correct understanding.
Amin.

2
PREFACE

BEFORE PRESENTING PROOFS for the permissibility of gathering for and celebrating the noble Prophetic nativity (*mawlid*), I want to clarify the following issues:

First, indeed, we say that it is permissible to celebrate the noble Prophetic nativity, congregating to hear his life story 鐮, listening to the praises that are due to him, serving food, and making the hearts of the Community (*umma*) happy.

Second, in reality, we do not say it is permissible to hold a yearly celebration of the Prophetic mawlid on a special designated night per se. Nay, whoever believes this has innovated in religion, because mentioning him 鐮 and connecting to him must be done at all times and must permeate our very souls. The month of his birth 鐮 is a potent factor for increasing people's receptiveness [to Islam], for bringing them together and activating their overflowing emotions by commemorating it in the same month, so they remember the past with the present, and move from the present day to the past [i.e. of the Prophetic era].

Third, these gatherings are an enormous means to invite people to Allah (*dawa*) and a golden opportunity that should not be missed. It is incumbent upon the callers to Allah (*duat*) and the scholars to remind the Muslim Community (*umma*) about the Prophet 鐮, his inward traits, his outward manners, his states, his biography, his social interactions and his worship [of Allah]. They must advise them and guide them to goodness and success, and warn them against calamities, innovations, evils and temptations. Truly, we always invite to that and take part in that.

We say to people, "The purpose of these gatherings is not merely 'to gather' or the 'outward manifestation'. Rather, this is a noble means to a noble end and it is such-and-such, and whoever does not take any benefit in this for their religion has been barred from all types of good found in the noble Mawlid".

3

Proofs for the Permissibility of Celebrating the Birth of the Prophet ﷺ

FIRST, the celebration of the noble Prophetic Mawlid is an expression of joy and happiness for the Chosen One (*al-mustafa*) ﷺ and this [joy] has even benefitted a disbeliever (*kafir*). Further explanation of this will come in the ninth proof. It should be noted that the foundational proof is one, with various methods of deduction. We have followed this methodology in this research and as such there is no undue repetition. It has come in Sahih al-Bukhari that the punishment will be lightened for Abu Lahab every Monday because he emancipated his servant girl Thuwayba ؓ when she gave him the good news of the birth of al-Mustafa ﷺ.

Al-Hafiz Shams al-Din, Muhammad b. Nasir al-Din al-Dimishqi comprised poetry about this:

إِذَا كَانَ هٰذَا كَافِرًا جَاءَ ذَمُّهُ بِتَبَّتْ يَدَاهُ فِي الْجَحِيمِ مُخَلَّدًا

أَتَى أَنَّهُ فِي يَوْمِ الْإِثْنَيْنِ دَائِمًا يُخَفَّفُ عَنْهُ لِلسُّرُورِ بِأَحْمَدًا

فَمَا الظَّنُّ بِالْعَبْدِ الَّذِي كَانَ عُمْرُهُ بِأَحْمَدٍ مَسْرُورًا وَمَاتَ مُوَحِّدًا

If this was about a disbeliever, whose blame has come with the destruction of his two hands, who is damned to the Hellfire for evermore (mukhallada)

It came about him that each and every Monday [his punishment] will be lightened because of his happiness towards Ahmad ﷺ

So what do you think about a slave, whom for his entire life was happy with Ahmad ﷺ and died believing in One God (muwahhida)

This report is recorded in:

- Imam Bukhari's sound compendium (*sahih*) in the chapter of 'marriage' (*nikah*) in *mursal*[2] fashion,
- Al-Hafiz Ibn Hajar's *Fath al-Bari*,
- Al-Imam Abd al-Razzaq al-Sanani's *al-Musannaf*,
- Al-Hafiz al-Bayhaqi's *al-Dalail al-Nabuwwa*,
- Ibn Kathir's *as-Sirah al-Nabawiyyah* from *al-Bidayah*,
- Muhammad b. Umar Bahriq's *Hada'iq al-Anwar*,
- Al-Hafiz al-Baghawi's *Sharh al-Sunnah*,
- Ibn Hisham and al-Suhayli's *al-Rawd al-Unuf*, and,
- Al-Amiri's *Bahjat al-Mahafil*.

Even though this report is *mursal*, it is acceptable because of its transmission by al-Bukhari, the reliance of master scholars of hadith (*Huffaz*) upon it, and its topic being related to virtues and special distinctions not to the permissible and prohibited (halal and haram). Even the students of Sacred knowledge know the difference between using ahadith to deduce proofs between virtues (*manaqib*) and rulings (*ahkam*).

As for the topic of disbelievers benefitting from their actions, there is academic discussion between the scholars about this, but this is not the place to expound on that. The foundation (*'asl*) of this is what was recorded in the Sahih about the lightening of the punishment of Abu Talib by the request of the Messenger ﷺ.

SECOND, he ﷺ used to honour the day of his birth, thank Allah ﷻ therein for the immense blessing upon him and Allah's favouring him ﷺ as a mercy for the entire universe, as everything in the world had the good fortune of receiving him ﷺ. He would express the greatness of this honour by fasting as was mentioned in the hadith from Abu Qatadah ﷺ which says that the Messenger of Allah ﷺ was asked about fasting on Mondays. He replied, "*On it, I was born, and*

---

[2] A *mursal* hadith is a hadith where the chain of narration goes up to a Successor of the Prophetic Companions (*tabii*). [t]

on it revelation descends upon me."[3] This corroborates the practice of celebrating him ﷺ except that the outward form differs, yet the meaning is the same. Even if it was by fasting or serving food, or gathering for remembering Allah (*dhikr*), or sending blessings (*salawat*) upon the Prophet ﷺ, or listening to his noble traits.

THIRD, happiness because of him ﷺ is desirable (*mustahabb*) by the Qur'anic injunction from the Word of Allah ﷻ, ❨*Say: In the bounty of Allah and in His Mercy—in that let them rejoice*❩[4] Allah Most High commanded us to show happiness because of His Mercy (*rahma*), and the Prophet ﷺ is the greatest *rahma*. Allah Most High said, ❨*And We have not sent you except as a mercy to all the worlds*❩[5]

FOURTH, the Prophet ﷺ would observe the connection between time and great Islamic events that have passed and expired. The recorded time of an event's occurrence is an opportunity to commemorate it, to magnify that day because of it, and because the day contained that event. The Prophet ﷺ himself founded this principle as explicitly stated in the authentic hadith that when he ﷺ arrived in Medina and he enquired about the Jews fasting on the Day of Ashura'. It was said to him that they fast because Allah saved their Prophet [Musa ﷺ] and drowned their enemy [Firawn], so they fast to show gratitude to Allah for this blessing. He then said ﷺ, "*We have more right to Musa ﷺ than you.*" So he fasted on that day and ordered others to fast on it too.

FIFTH, the noble Mawlid revives and awakens blessings and salutations on the Prophet ﷺ; two desirable things shown in Allah Most High's words, ❨*Verily, Allah and His angels send blessings on the Prophet: O you who believe! Send blessings on him, and salute him with a worthy salutation*❩[6] Whatever prompts one to perform what is desirable by the Sacred Law (*shariah*) is in itself desirable

---

[3] Narrated by Imam Muslim in his *Sahih* in the Chapter of Fasting. [t]
[4] Qur'an 10:58
[5] Qur'an 21:107
[6] Qur'an 33:56

by the Sacred Law. How numerous are the benefits for sending blessings upon the Prophet ﷺ, and how much Muhammadan support does one receive? The pen prostrates in the prayer-niche (*mihrab*) of elucidation, incapable of enumerating its effects and manifesting its lights.

SIXTH, the noble Mawlid contains mention of his noble birth ﷺ, his miracles, his biography, and learning about him. Are we not commanded to know him ﷺ, required to follow him ﷺ, to base our actions on his actions, bring faith (*iman*) in his miracles, and to confirm his signs? The books of the Mawlid fulfil this meaning completely.

SEVENTH, it attempts to show our appreciation and fulfils some of what we owe to him ﷺ through discussing his qualities of perfection and virtuous character. The poets would pay homage to him with religious poems (*qasa'id*) and he ﷺ was pleased with their actions. He would reward them for that with good things and prayers. If he ﷺ was pleased with those who praised him, then how would he not be pleased with those who compiled his noble qualities? Thus, in doing so, one is attaining closeness to him ﷺ by attracting his love and pleasure.

EIGHTH, knowing his traits, his miracles (*mu'jizat*), and his miracles before prophethood (*irhasat*), summons one to bring complete faith (*iman*) in him ﷺ and increase in love for him. Humans are naturally attracted to beautiful things, and there is nothing more beautiful, more perfect, and more virtuous than his manners (*akhlaq*) and qualities (*shama'il*) ﷺ. Increased love for him and perfect iman are two desirable things in the Sacred Law (*shariah*), so whatever will result in these two things is equally desirable.

NINTH, respect for him ﷺ is legislated by the Sacred Law (*shariah*), and feeling joy on the day of his noble birth by showing happiness, preparing feasts, gathering for the remembrance of Allah (*dhikr*) and treating the poor hospitably are from the most obvious ways to show reverence, happiness and thankfulness to Allah for guiding us to His upright religion, and what He favoured us with through him ﷺ since his advent (upon him be the choicest prayers and peace).

TENTH, it is taken from his word ﷺ on the virtues of the Day of Jumua and its special features, *"In it, Prophet Adam ﷺ was created"*, and in honour of the established time, that is the birth [origin] of every single prophet from the Prophets ﷺ. So how about the day of birth of the best of the Prophets and the most noble of the Messengers ﷺ?

This honouring is not designated to the day of his birth specifically. Rather, it is specifically celebrated in that day, and generally celebrated in other days, regardless of its repetition, much like the Day of Jumua, out of thankfulness for the blessing, manifesting his prophetic superiority ﷺ, and reviving this significant historic event which was healing in its nature, important in the history of mankind, prominent in time immemorial, and a page of history that is immortal.

The greatness of the birthplace of a prophet was taken as important when Jibril ﷺ request that the Prophet ﷺ pray two *raka* at Bethlehem (Ar. *bayt al-laham*); Jibril ﷺ said to him ﷺ, *"Do you know where you prayed?"* He ﷺ replied, *"No"*. He said, *"You prayed at Bethlehem where 'Isa ﷺ was born"*, as it came in the hadith of Shaddad b. Aws ﷺ, narrated by al-Bazzar and Abu Yala and al-Tabarani. Al-Hafiz al-Haythami said in *Majma al-Zawaid* its narrators are authentic and al-Hafiz b. Hajar transmitted this narration in his *Fath al-Bari* and was silent about it.

ELEVENTH, the Mawlid is an issue scholars have deemed to be good along with the Muslims of all countries. It has been practiced in every region, thus it is desirable according to the Sacred Law (*shariah*) by the principle taken from the *mawquf*[7] hadith of Ibn Masud ﷺ stating, *"What the Muslims deem to be good is good with*

---

[7] A *mawquf* hadith is a statement attributed to a Prophetic Companion (*sahabi*). [t]

41

Allah, and what the Muslims deem to be bad is bad with Allah."[8]

TWELFTH, the Mawlid comprises of gathering, remembering Allah (*dhikr*), charity, praises, and reverence of his Prophetic Eminence ﷺ, thus it is fulfilling a Sunnah. These issues are desirable and praiseworthy in the Sacred Law and authentic sayings have come regarding them and encouraging them.

THIRTEENTH, Allah Most High said, ⟪*And each [incident] We relate to you from the news of the Messengers by which We make firm your heart*⟫[9] So this verse from Him ﷻ makes it clear that the wisdom (*hikma*) in relating the news of the [prior] Messengers is to strengthen (*tathbit*) his noble heart with it. There is no doubt that we today, are in more need to strengthen our hearts with his news and stories than his need ﷺ.

FOURTEENTH, it is not incumbent to reject everything the pious predecessors did not do, or that were not in the first generation of Islam. The absence of these actions does not make them evil and reprehensible innovations as a matter of course. Rather, it is obligatory to assess any 'new' actions against the foundations of the Sacred Law. That which consists of what is beneficial (*maslahah*) is deemed necessary and of what is prohibited is deemed prohibited, or of the disliked (*makruh*) is deemed *makruh*, or of the permissible (*mubah*) is deemed *mubah*, or of the recommended (*mandub*) is deemed *mandub*. The means has the same ruling as the end.

---

[8] Recorded by Imam Ahmad.
[9] Qur'an 11:120

42

FIFTEENTH, not every innovation (*bidah*)[10] is prohibited. Were it so, then it would have:

- Prohibited Abu Bakr, 'Umar and Zaid ﷺ from collating the Qur'an.
- Prevented Zaid's recording the Qur'an in book form out of fear of it being lost by the death of the memorizers (*huffaz*) among the Companions (*sahaba*) ﷺ.
- Prohibited Umar ﷺ from gathering the people to pray night prayers (*salat al-qiyam*) behind one Imam, with his word, "*What a blessed innovation (bidah) this is.*"
- Prohibited the authoring of books in every beneficial form of knowledge.
- Meant we had to militarily engage the disbelievers with bows and arrows despite them fighting us with bullets, machine guns, tanks, airplanes, submarines and fleets.
- Prohibited to raise the call to prayer (*adhan*) on the minarets (*mana'ir*).
- Prohibited the development of military forts, schools, hospitals, ambulances, orphanages and prisons.

From this viewpoint, the scholars ﷺ have restricted the hadith, "*Every innovation (bidah) is misguidance*", to apply only to reprehensible innovations. This restriction is explained by referencing examples from the Companions and the Successors ﷺ of innovations that did not happen in the Prophet's time ﷺ. Similarly, we today, have introduced many new matters that the pious predecessors (*salaf*) did not do, such as:

---

[10] FIVE CATEGORIES OF INNOVATION: Scholars have categorized innovation into five:
- NECESSARY (*wajib*): like refuting deviant groups and learning grammar.
- RECOMMENDED (*mustahab*): like creating Islamic military forts and schools, the call to prayer on the minarets (*mana'ir*), and doing [any] act of excellence that was not present in the first stage of Islam.
- PERMISSIBLE (*halal*): like using a sieve, or having variety in food and drink.
- DISLIKED (*makruh*): like decorating the masjid and embellishing the Qur'an (*mushaf*).
- PROHIBITED (*haram*): what occurs that is contrary to the Sunnah, is not in accordance to the general foundational proofs of the Sacred Law, or does not concur with the benefits of the Sacred Law.

- Assembling people behind one Imam in the last portion of the night for *salat al-tahajjud* after *salat al-tarawih,*
- Completing the Qur'an therein,
- Reciting the special *dua'* when completing the Qur'an,
- The Imam's sermon (*khutbah*) on the 27th night at *salat al-tahajjud,*
- The announcer calling out, "*Night vigil prayer! May Allah reward you.*"[11]

All of this was not done by the Prophet ﷺ nor anyone from the *salaf,* but is our performing these actions a reprehensible innovation?

SIXTEENTH, celebrating the Mawlid, as it was not done in his time ﷺ, is indeed an innovation; but, it is a 'good innovation' because it is encompassed within the foundational proofs of the Sacred Law and the principles in their totality. It is an innovation with respect to collective celebration, but not with respect to its being marked as a day to celebrate, due to it being marked in the Prophetic era, which is understood in the twelfth proof.

SEVENTEENTH, everything that was not present in the first era of Islam in a collective form, but was individually present, is desirable by the Sacred Law because what consists of things compliant with the Sacred Law is in accordance to the Sacred Law, which is no secret.

EIGHTEENTH, Imam al-Shafi'i ﷺ said, "*What is newly-introduced and opposes the Book or the Sunnah or scholarly consensus (ijma') or deductive-analogy (qiyas) or narration is a misguided innovation; and any good (khayr) that is introduced and does not oppose anything from the above-mentioned is praiseworthy.*"

---

[11] This occurs nightly at the two of the three Holy Sanctuaries, namely Mecca al-Mukarrama and Medina al-Munawwara. [t]

Imam al-Izz b. 'Abd al-Salam, al-Nawawi and likewise Ibn al-Athir have gone on to divide innovation into the categories we indicated previously.[12]

NINETEENTH, all good that aligns with foundational proofs in the Sacred Law, is not intended to oppose the Sacred Law and does not consist of the reprehensible, is included in the religion.

The zealous phrase, "*This was not done by the pious predecessors*", is not a proof against any action. It is actually defined as the absence of a proof as understood by anyone who has undertaken even a cursory study of the knowledge of foundational principles (*ilm al-usul*). Indeed, the Sacred Law has classified a 'guided innovation' as Sunnah and promised its doer a reward.

Like the Messenger of Allah ﷺ said, "*Whoever initiates a good Sunnah in Islam, and people act according to it after him, a copy of the reward is recorded for him equivalent to the one who acted upon it without decreasing their rewards at all.*"

TWENTIETH, the celebration of the Prophetic Mawlid is reviving the mention of the Chosen One (*al-mustafa*) ﷺ which is legislated by the Sacred Law for us in Islam. You yourself see that the majority of the rites of Hajj consist of the honouring of memorable events and praiseworthy places. The jogging (*sai*) between Safa and Marwa, stoning (*rami*) of the pillars (*jamarat*), and sacrificing an animal in Mina, are all events of the past. The Muslims revive these memories by re-enacting Hajj rituals in the present day. The proof for that is the Word of Allah Most High, ❨*And proclaim among mankind the Pilgrimage (Hajj)*❩[13] and Allah's Words speaking about the incident of Prophet Ibrahim ﷺ and Prophet Ismail ﷺ ❨*...and show us our rites of worship*❩[14]

---

[12] For more information, please see Appendix II on the correct use of weak hadith. [t]
[13] Qur'an 22:27
[14] Qur'an 2:128

TWENTY-FIRST, all that we have mentioned previously of the perspectives on the legality of the Mawlid is only addressing the Mawlid that is free from reprehensible and blameworthy acts that must be rejected.

As for the Mawlid that consists of things that must be rejected like mixing of men and women, committing the forbidden (*haram*), abundant wastefulness (*israf*) that does not please the Prophet 🌸 (*sahib al-mawlid*), then without doubt, that would be forbidden. That which comprises of the forbidden is not allowed. However, its prohibition at that time is conditional, not intrinsic to the Mawlid, which is no secret to the one who reflects upon it.

4

THE OPINION OF SHAYKH IBN TAYMIYYA ON THE MAWLID

HE SAYS, "*Some people may be rewarded for performing the Mawlid. Similarly, what some people recant about either resembling the Christians in the birth of 'Isa ﷺ or out of love for the Prophet ﷺ and honouring him, Allah may reward them for this love and striving (ijtihad), not [punish them] for innovation.*"

Then he said, "*Know that there are actions that are good because they contain a variety of things legislated by the Sacred Law and also, there are evil innovations and other than that. So that action is deemed evil because of its conflict to the religion in a holistic sense like the state of the hypocrites and the corrupt. This has been a trial for the majority of the Umma in recent times.*"

"*So hold fast to two manners, the first of which is, to see to it that you and those legally obliged to obey you are avid in holding fast to the Sunnah inwardly and outwardly, and enjoin what is right and forbid what is wrong. Secondly, invite people to the Sunnah as much as possible. If you see someone doing wrong and he will not abandon it except to do worse than it, then do not invite him to leave that wrong if it will result in him doing what is worse than it, or result in him abandoning the necessary (wajib) or recommended (mustahab). The individual abandoning the necessary (wajib) is more harmful than him performing the disliked (makruh). However, if there was a type of good in an innovation, then substitute it for him with a type of good that complies with the Sacred Law as much as possible because souls do not abandon something except for something else. No one should abandon something good except for something equivalent to it or what is better than it.*"

He goes on to say: "*Honouring the Mawlid and taking it as a season the way some people do will reap an immense reward because of their virtuous goal and their reverence for Allah's Messenger ﷺ as I mentioned to you, [namely] that some things are deemed good for some people that would be deemed reprehensible for a strong believer (mu'min).*"

It was said to Imam Ahmad ﷺ about one of the leaders that he spent 1,000 dinars (gold coins) on a copy of the Qur'an (*mushaf*) and the like. He replied, "*Leave him, for this is the best thing gold can be spent for*", or he said similar to that, even though in his madhab, the decorating of the mushaf is disliked (*makruh*). Some of the scholars have explained that the leader spent it to restore the pages and writing. This was not the intent of [the dislike of] Imam Ahmad, rather his intent was that, this action does have benefit, but also corruption in it. It is for that reason it is disliked.

5

THE UNDERSTANDING OF THE MAWLID IN MY OPINION

ACCORDING TO US, celebrating the noble Prophetic Mawlid does not have a specific method that must be adhered to or that people must be made to abide by. Rather, everything that invites to good, gathers people upon guidance (*hidaya*), instructs them to what is in their best interest regarding their religion and worldly affairs actually fulfils the goal of the Prophetic Mawlid.

Some may consider the Prophetic Mawlid incomplete if we neglect to recite a story that people have become so accustomed to, that they consider it integral. We may gather to mention praises (*madh*) that contain the mention of the Beloved (*al-Habib*) ﷺ, his virtue, his battles (*jihad*), his distinctions (*khasa'is*). Thereafter, we may listen carefully to what the scholars of hadith (*muhaddithun*) have presented of admonitions and instructions, and to what is recited by a proficient reciter (*qari'*) from the verses of the Qur'an.

I say: If we did that, then indeed that enters under the noble Prophetic Mawlid [even if we did not recite a particular story], and is achieving the meaning of celebrating the noble Prophetic Mawlid. I believe no two people will disagree with this meaning, nor will they butt heads about it.

6

STANDING IN THE MAWLID

AS FOR STANDING in the Prophetic Mawlid when his birth 🕌 and his emergence into the world is mentioned; verily, some people have ideas about this that have no basis with the people of knowledge, according to what I know, and are completely incorrect. These ideas, that people are standing, believing that the Prophet 🕌 is entering into their gathering at that very moment with his noble body, or that the incensed-wood (*bakhur*) and perfume (*tib*) is for him 🕌 and the water that is put in the middle of the gathering is for him 🕌 to drink from, are erroneous and would not even cross the mind of an intelligent Muslim. Rather, even the most ignorant people that attend the Mawlid and join with those who stand know this is not the case. Truly, we exonerate ourselves with Allah from all that occurs regarding the status of Allah's Messenger 🕌 and the false assertions about his noble body [at the Mawlid] which none believe save a godless fabricator. No one knows about the affairs of the life in the grave (*barzakh*) except Allah Most High.

The Prophet 🕌 is too lofty, perfect and majestic for it to be said about him that he leaves his grave and attends such-and-such gathering at such-and-such time in bodily form. I say that this is unadulterated falsehood that contains such audacity, insolence, and foulness, it can only come from a malicious hater or a stubborn ignoramus.

Yes, indeed we do believe that he 🕌 is living in the perfect life of the intermediary realm (*barzakh*) as is befitting his status. In accordance with that lofty perfect form of life, his soul is able to travel and roam in the realm of the unseen dominion (*malakut*) of Allah 🕌 and it is possible that it be present at gatherings of good and places of light (*nur*) and knowledge (*'ilm*), as is possible for the pure souls of the believers from his followers. Indeed, Imam Malik ﷺ has said, "*It has reached me that the soul is sent-forth, going wherever it wishes.*"

Salman al-Farisi ﷺ said, "*The souls of believers are in the barzakh of the earth. They go wherever they will*". Ibn al-Qayyim ﷺ recorded it as such in his book '*The Soul*' (*ar-Ruh*).

So now that you know this, then know that standing in the Prophetic Mawlid is not necessary (*wajib*) nor Sunnah, and to believe that is incorrect. It is an action done by people expressing their happiness and joy. When it is mentioned that the Messenger of Allah ﷺ was born and came into the world, the listener pictures that the entire universe shook in happiness and joy by this blessing, so stands to show his/her happiness. Thus, it is purely an act of custom or convention, not religion.

7

THE SCHOLARS DEEMING THE STANDING OF THE MAWLID TO BE GOOD AND EXPLAINING THE REASONING BEHIND IT

INDEED, standing in the Mawlid is not worship (*ibada*), commanded by the Sacred Law, or Sunnah; it is simply a custom that has been deemed good by the people of knowledge (*ahl al-ilm*). It has been indicated by Imam al-Barzanji ﷺ, himself an author of one of the *Mawalid*, when he said in the text:

> *Standing when the noble birth is mentioned has been deemed good by Imams of narrations and erudition. So glad tidings to the one whose ultimate desire and aspiration is honouring him* ﷺ

What we mean by 'deeming something good' here is that it is intrinsically permissible and its foundation is praiseworthy and desirable in the Sacred Law, from its motivations to its outcomes; not the technical meaning of 'good' used in the foundational principles (*usul al-fiqh*). Even the student with the least knowledge knows that the phrase 'deem good' is used in mundane affairs amongst people. So they say, 'I deem this book to be good' or 'this is a good matter' or 'or people deem this act to be good'. Their whole intent in this is linguistically and commonly deeming something good. Otherwise, by default the affairs of people have Sacred Law rulings, and no intelligent person or anyone familiar with juristic principles (*usul*) would suggest this.

8

THE REASONS BEHIND DEEMING STANDING TO BE GOOD

FIRST, this action has been in practice in all regions and cities and has been deemed good by scholars in the east and the west. Its intention is to honour the noble Mawlid of the Messenger of Allah ﷺ. What the Muslims deem good is deemed good by Allah and what the Muslims deem bad is deemed bad by Allah, as established by the preceding hadith.

SECOND, standing for people of virtue is legislated by the Sacred Law, and firmly established by many proofs from the Sunnah. Imam al-Nawawi ﷺ has authored an independent chapter about this, and Ibn Hajar ﷺ has supported him and wrote a refutation to Ibn al-Hajj ﷺ, who opposed standing, with another volume entitled, 'Removing the blame from the one who deem standing to be good'.

THIRD, as reported in the agreed upon hadith, the Prophet ﷺ said to the Ansar, "Stand for your master" (qumu ila sayyidikum) referring to Sa'd ibn Muadh ﷺ. The command to stand was in order to honour our master and not because he was sick; for if it were due to sickness he ﷺ would have said 'stand for your sick one', not 'your master'. He did not order all people to stand; rather he only ordered some.

FOURTH, it was from the Prophet's guidance ﷺ to stand in honour for one entering upon him to create a good relationship, just as he stood for our Lady Fatima ﷺ and approved of her showing reverence to him by doing the same. So too, he ordered the Ansar to stand for their master. This indicates the permissibility in the Sacred Law of standing, and he ﷺ has more right to be honoured in that regard.

FIFTH, it could be argued, "*That only applies in his lifetime ﷺ and in his presence, and at the time of the Mawlid gathering he is not present.*" The one reciting the noble Mawlid is calling him to mind by envisioning his noble essence ﷺ, which is praiseworthy and desirable. It is incumbent for every true Muslim to give all of one's attention to the Messenger of Allah ﷺ, at all times, to perfect one's following of him ﷺ, increase one's love for him, and to strive to make one's desires in accordance with what he brought. People stand out of respect and esteem for the vivid image in their hearts of the persona of this grand Messenger ﷺ, feeling the majesty and greatness even though standing is a mundane thing, as we mentioned. This envisioning by the one remembering the Prophet ﷺ is a cause for an increase in reverence for the Messenger of Allah ﷺ.

9
BOOKS AUTHORED
ON THIS TOPIC

THE BOOKS AUTHORED ABOUT THIS TOPIC are remarkably abundant; some versified (arranged like a poem), some in prose, some summarized, some lengthy, and some medium in length. We do not want, in this brief treatise, to mention the entire corpus because of its abundance and vastness. Likewise, we are not able to mention a short list, in a brief summary, because one book is not better than another in order to prioritize its mention, even though, of course, some are better and more impressive than others. Therefore, I will suffice to mention some great scholars of the *umma*, who were *huffaz* among the Imams, that authored works on this topic, and the famous and well-known *Mawalid* that they produced.

AL-HAFIZ IBN NASIR AL-DIN AL-DIMISHQI

Hafiz Muhammad b. Abu Bakr b. Abdillah al-Qisi al-Dimishqi al-Shafi'i famously known as *Hafiz Ibn Nasir al-Din al-Dimishqi* was born in the year 777 AH and died in year 842 AH. It is said about him by Hafiz Ibn Fahd in *Lahz al-Alhaz* at the end of *Tadhkirat al-Huffaz* on page 319, *"He is the Imam, the beneficial Hafiz, the exalted historian; he has a pure, sound and accurate mind, enjoyable and beautiful writing following the way of the scholars of hadith."* He said, *"His books are abundant, commented on, made notes of, verified, printed, became prominent to his peers, and have benefitted whoever sought them out."*

The Sheikh was appointed as a manager at Dar al-Hadith al-Ashrafia in Damascus. Imam al-Suyuti 🕮 said about him, *"He became the Muhaddith of Damascus."* Shaykh Muhammad Zahid said in his commentary at the end of the biographies *(tabaqat)*, *"Al-Hafiz Jamal al-Din b. Abd al-Hadi al-Hanbali said in his book 'The Fruitful Garden' (Riyad al-Yan'iah) about the biography of the aforementioned Ibn Nasir al-Din 'The respected Shaykh Ibn Taymiyya loved him and had deep affection for him.'"*

Ibn Fahd mentioned that he authored a book entitled *'The Ample Refutation of he who alleged that Ibn Taymiyya Shaykh al-Islam was a Disbeliever.'* I say, this Imam has authored numerous volumes on the Noble Mawlid, the titles of some of which were mentioned by the author of *Kashf al-Zunun 'an Asami al-Kutub wa al-Funun* (p. 319), *"...and Jami' al-Athar fi Mawlid al-Nabi al-Mukhtar in three volumes, and al-Lafz al-Ra'iq fi Mawlid Khayr al-Khala'iq, which is an abridged work..."* Ibn Fahd said, *"He also authored Mawrid al-Sawi fi Mawlid al-Hadi."*

AL-HAFIZ AL-'IRAQI

Hafiz 'Abd al-Rahim b. Husain b. 'Abd al-Rahman al-Misri famously known as *al-Hafiz al-'Iraqi* was born in the year 725 AH and died in 808 AH. He is the great famous Imam Abu al-Fadl Zain al-Din, unparalleled in his time and unique in his era, *Hafiz al-Islam*, the one creatures relied upon, the learned, the proof, and the learned critic. He was superior in memory and excellence in his time, and the Imams of his time testified that he was unsurpassed in his field. He was proficient in hadith, chain of narration *(isnad)*, memorization *(hifz)* and mastery *(itqan)*. He became someone who the Egyptian Fatwa Council was known to consult.

So what can I say about an Imam like this, a vast ocean, a paragon of the outstanding stars of the Sunnah, a massive mountain from among the pillars of this upright religion? It suffices us that the scholars accept his word in hadith, chains of transmission, and nomenclature, and refer back to him when it is said 'al-Iraqi'. In this subject matter his *Alfiya* [a one thousand line compilation on the science of hadith] is relied upon; and anyone with the slightest bit of knowledge in, and connection to hadith, acknowledges his virtue and mastery. Indeed, this Imam has authored a noble Mawlid named *'The wholesome watering place on the lofty Mawlid.'* More than one of the *huffaz* have vouched for his books such as Ibn Fahd and al-Suyuti in their commentaries on the *Tadhkirah*.

AL-HAFIZ AL-SAKHAWI

Hafiz Muhammad 'Abd al-Rahman b. Muhammad al-Qahiri more famously known as *al-Hafiz al-Sakhawi* was born in 831 AH and died in 902 AH in Medina Munawwara; he is the great historian and the famous *Hafiz*.

Imam al-Shawkani ﷺ wrote about him in a biography in 'al-Badr al-Tali' saying, *"He is from the great Imams."* Ibn Fahd ﷺ said, *"I did not see amongst the later huffaz the likes of him. He has an abundance of gnosis, knowledge of the narrators of hadith, knowledge of the states of the narrators, knowledge about the science of criticizing and praising narrators of hadith (jarh and taadil), and he is consulted therein until some of the scholars said, 'No one has come after Hafiz al-Dhahabi like him and tread this path as he did. After him the science of hadith died.'"*

Al-Shawkani ﷺ said: *"Even if he had not authored a single book other than 'al-'Daw al-Lami', it in and of itself would have been the sufficient proof of his leadership (Imamat)"*. I say, he said in *Kashf al-Zunun*, *"Indeed al-Hafiz al-Sakhawi authored a work on the noble Mawlid ﷺ."*

MULLA 'ALI AL-QARI

Hafiz, Mujtahid, Imam Mulla 'Ali al-Qari b. Sultan b. Muhammad al-Harawi died in 1014 AH, the author of the commentary of *al-Mishkat* and other works.

Imam al-Shawkani ﷺ wrote a biography on him in *al-Badr al-Tali* saying, *"Al-'Isami said describing him [al-Qari], 'He gathered the knowledge of narrations, was skilled in the Prophet's Sunnah, one of the learned men by consensus, famous for his strong memory* and understanding.'" Then he said, "However, he was subjected to tribulations by opposing the Imams, especially Imam al-Shafi'i." Then al-Shawkani took it upon himself to protect and defend Mulla Ali al-Qari 🙭 after reproducing the words of al-'Isami by saying, "I say this is a proof towards his lofty rank, for truly, the role of a Mujtahid is to clarify what opposes authentic proofs, regardless of whether the speaker is prominent or insignificant. This is a complaint, the blameworthiness of which, is obvious."

This *Mujtahid Muhaddith Imam*, whom Imam al-Shawkani discussed in his biography, has authored a book on the Mawlid of Rasulullah 🙠. The author of *Kashf al-Zunun* said, "Its name is 'The watering place of the thirsty about the prophetic Mawlid.'" I have edited it, by Allah's bounty, and made a commentary on it and printed it for the first time.

IBN KATHIR AL-SHAFI'I

Hafiz Imad al-Din, Ismail b. 'Umar b. Kathir, the author of the tafsir. Imam al-Dhahabi 🙭 said about his features, "*The Imam, Mufti, Muhaddith, skillful, reliable, master of several types of knowledge, and God-fearing.*"

It is related from al-Shihab Ahmad Ibn Hajar al-Asqalani 🙭 in *al-Durar al-Kaminah* on page 374, "*He occupied himself with researching the texts (mutun) of hadith and its narrators (rijal).*" He said, "*He took from Ibn Taymiyya 🙭 and was put into tribulation because of loving him and was tested because of him. He was always known for being fun-loving and lighthearted. His works became widespread in the land in his lifetime, and people benefitted from them after his death in 744 AH.*" *Imam* Ibn Kathir 🙭 authored a prophetic Mawlid that was recently published, edited by Dr Salah al-Din al-Munajjad.

IBN DAYBA AL-YAMANI AL-ZABIDI

Hafiz Wajih al-Din 'Abd ar-Rahman b. 'Ali b. Muhammad al-Shaybani al-Yamani al-Zabidi al-Shafi'i, famously known as Ibn

Dayba. Dayba means 'white' in the Sudanese language; it is a nickname of his grandfather ʿAli b. Yusuf. He was born in Muharram in 866 AH and died on Jumua on the 12th of Rajab, the solitary, in the year 944 AH. He 🙼 was one of the scholars of his time, was the foremost master in the science of hadith and taught the Sahih of al-Bukhari more than 100 times. Once he recited it in six days.

He authored a Prophetic Mawlid that is famous in many countries, and we edited it and commented on it and made references for its *ahadith* by the Grace of Allah.

[Shaykh] MUHAMMAD ʿALAWI AL-MALIKI AL-HASANI
The servant of sacred knowledge in the land of Allah
THE MECCAN SANCTUARY

Standing During the Mawlid
Remarks by Habib Umar bin Hafiz

مَا حُكْمُ الْقِيَامِ بِذِكْرِ مَدْحِ النَّبِيِّ صَلَّى اللهُ عَلَيْهِ وَسَلَّمَ ؟

أَلْقِيَامُ فِي الشَّرِيعَةِ الْغَرَّاءِ لَا يُحْرُمُ إِلَّا لِلْمُحَرَّمِ ، قَدْ أَنْ يَكُونَ لِنِيَّةِ تَعْظِيمِ لِكُفْرِ كَافِرٍ أَوْ فُجُورِ فَاجِرٍ أَوْ يَكُونَ فِي مُشَارَكَةِ صَاحِبِ الْمَعْصِيَةِ فِي مَعْصِيَتِهِ أَوْ يَقُومَ لِيَفْعَلَ مُحَرَّمًا ، فَمَا وَرَاءَ ذَلِكَ فَلَوْ أَرَادَ الْإِنْسَانُ أَنْ يَقُومَ أَوْ يَقْعُدَ عِشْرِينَ مَرَّةٍ أَوْ ثَلَاثِينَ مَرَّةٍ مَثَلًا فَلَا شَيْءُ فِي شَرِيعَةِ اللهِ يَنْهَهُ عَنْ ذَلِكَ .

فَأَمَّا إِنْ كَانَ يَقْصُدُ جَمْعَ بَيْنَ الذِّكْرِ قِيَامًا وَقُعُودًا فَهَذَا مَقْصُودٌ شَرِيفٌ ، وَأَمَّا إِنْ كَانَ يَقْصُدُ إِظْهَارَ الْفَرَحِ بِذِكْرِ وِلَادَةِ النَّبِيِّ مُحَمَّدٍ إِذَا ذُكِرَتْ وِلَادَتُهُ قَامَ تَعْبِيرًا عَنِ الْفَرَحِ وَتَعْظِيمِ لِرَسُولِ اللهِ فَهَذَا مِنْ عَظِيمِ قُرُبَاتِ إِلَى اللهِ ، فَهَلْ يَجُوزُ الْقِيَامَ لِأَيِّ شَيْءٍ وَلَوْ أُرِيدُ أَنْ أَتَنَاوَلَ مَتَاعً أَوْ أَهْدِيَةً إِلَّا عِنْدَ ذِكْرِ وِلَادَةِ رَسُولٍ يُحْرُمُ؟

ثُمَّ إِنَّ الْقِيَامَ لِأَجْلِ إِكْرَامِ أَحَدٍ إِنْ كَانَ ذَلِكَ مُكَرَّمٌ مُسْلِمًا فَلَا حَرَجَ فِيهِ ، وَإِنْ كَانَ ذَلِكَ مُكَرَّمٌ مُتَجَاهِرٌ بِالْفِسْقِ أَوْ مُتَظَاهِرٌ بِالْكُفْرِ فَلَا يَجُوزُ لِأَنَّ ذَلِكَ لَا يَجُوزُ .

What is the ruling of standing when the Prophet's praises are mentioned ﷺ?

Standing in the radiant Sacred Law is not forbidden unless you are standing for something forbidden. This [forbidden standing] may occur when someone stands intending to honour the disbelief of a disbeliever, or the corruption of a profligate, or standing to partake in the disobedience of a disobedient person, or the person stands to do something prohibited (*haram*). Otherwise if someone wants to stand up or sit down twenty or thirty times, for example, then there is nothing in the Sacred Law of Allah to prohibit someone from doing that.

As for when a person intends by this to join between standing and remembering Allah, then this is a noble aim. If they intend by standing, [to show] joy and reverence at the mention of the birth of the Prophet ﷺ and so that they stand as an expression of this joy and reverence, then that is included among the greatest acts we can do to draw nearer to Allah. So is it permissible to stand for anything like getting anything, or picking up shoes, and the only time it is forbidden to stand is when the birth of the Messenger ﷺ is mentioned?

Thereafter, standing in honour of someone, if the one being honoured is Muslim, contains no harm therein. But, if the one being honoured is proudly committing corruption or openly manifesting disbelief and one stands due to that quality, then that is prohibited.

March 20th, 2011 at I.M.O. Masjid
Toronto, CANADA

The Correct Use of Weakly Authenticated Hadith

THE SLOGAN 'QUR'AN AND SUNNAH' has been repeated to the Muslim masses so much that it has become wrongly interpreted to mean 'only' the Qur'an and Sunnah should be followed without qualified scholarship. Whilst they are the two primary sources of Islamic law, the other two being analogy (*qiyas*) and scholarly consensus (*ijma*), there are so many innovations (*bidah*) folded within this catch phrase that the common Muslim may not understand. One of them being our topic here about the proper use of the weak hadith of the Messenger of Allah ﷺ.

Many people claim, and make others feel, that it is impermissible and not allowed to follow weak hadith; they themselves feel fear and create in others fear, uncertainty and anxiety about any book that has any weakly authenticated hadith in it. A cursory glance at the works on the science of hadith reveal that it is actually permissible to follow weakly authenticated hadith in all matters except for the permissible and prohibited (*halal* and *haram*). For example, those hadith that encourage us to do what we know is halal (lawful) like reciting 100 benedictions (*salat as-salam*) on the Messenger of Allah ﷺ on Fridays, or discourage us from doing what we know is prohibited like lying, speaking about Islam without knowledge, or cheating.

AL-NAWAWI'S STATEMENT ON WEAKLY AUTHENTICATED HADITH

The great Shafi'i Imam, the *Hafiz* of Hadith, author of the famous *Riyad al-Salihin*, the *zahid* (ascetic), and *faqih* (jurist), the Syrian Imam al-Nawawi ﷺ has mentioned this point in several places in his various works. In the introduction to his *Kitab al-Adhkar* he states:

قَالَ الْعُلَمَاءُ مِنَ الْمُحَدِّثِيْنَ وَالْفُقَهَاءِ وَغَيْرِهِمْ : يَجُوْزُ وَيَسْتَحَبُّ الْعَمَلُ فِي
فَضَائِلِ وَالتَّرْغِيْبِ وَالتَّرْهِيْبِ بِالْحَدِيْثِ الضَّعِيْفِ مَا لَمْ يَكُنْ مَوْضُوْعًا .

The scholars of the hadith (*muhaddithun*) and the jurists (*fuqaha*) and others declared, "*It is permissible and praiseworthy (mustahabb) to act upon weak hadith to do good deeds (fadail), in encouragement of good (al-targhib) and preventing evil (al-tarhib) with a weak hadith as long as the hadith is not forged.*"[15]

Today, some people claim that a weak hadith is, in essence, like a forged hadith and that under no circumstances can we follow it. As if this was not bad enough, they go so far as to insist that it is impermissible to mention a weak hadith without mentioning that it is weak. However, while it is impermissible (*haram*) to follow or even mention a forged hadith without mentioning that it is forged, that is not the case with weak hadith.

HOW SHOULD ONE MENTION WEAKLY AUTHENTICATED HADITH?

When mentioning a weak hadith one should not say "*The Messenger of Allah ﷺ said …*", but rather should say, "*It is reported that the Messenger of Allah ﷺ said …*", or something similar, that does not positively affirm that the report is a statement of the Prophet ﷺ.

IMAM AL-SUYUTI COMMENTING ON IMAM AL-NAWAWI'S STATEMENT ON REPORTING WEAK HADITH

To make this clear, among the great authorities in the science of hadith were Imam al-Nawawi and Imam al-Suyuti. Here follows a statement of Imam al-Nawawi ﷺ from his book on the principles of the science of hadith (*usul al-hadith*), known as *al-Taqrib* with the celebrated commentary (*sharh*) of Imam al-Suyuti from Imam al-Suyuti's *Tadrib al-Rawi*. This commentary is now recognized as a textbook and primary resource on the principles of the science of hadith.

The text from al-Nawawi is in **bold type** while al-Suyuti's interpolations are in regular type and there are a few of my own

---

[15] *Kitab al-Adhkar*, al-Nawawi, page 7. Dar al-Kutub al-'Ilmiyah, Beirut. [t]

interpolations which I have distinguished by placing them within square brackets:

وَيَجُوزُ عِنْدَ أَهْلِ الْحَدِيثِ وَغَيْرِهِمُ التَّسَاهُلَ فِي الْأَسَانِيدِ الضَّعِيفَةِ وَرِوَايَةَ مَا سِوَى الْمَوْضُوعُ مِنَ الضَّعِيفِ وَالْعَمَلَ بِهِ مِنْ غَيْرِ بَيَانِ ضَعْفِهِ فِي غَيْرِ صِفَاتِ اللهِ تَعَالَى وَمَا يَجُوزُ وَيَسْتَحِيلُ عَلَيْهِ وَتَفْسِيرَ كَلَامِهِ وَالْأَحْكَامَ كَالْحَلَالِ وَالْحَرَامِ وَ غَيْرِهِمَا وَذَلِكَ كَالْقَصَصِ وَفَضَائِلِ الْأَعْمَالِ وَالْمَوَاعِظِ وَغَيْرِهَا مِمَّا لَا تَعَلَّقَ لَهُ بِالْعَقَائِدِ وَالْأَحْكَامِ .

According to the authorities in the field of hadith and other fields, it is allowed to be lenient with respect to:

1. The chains of transmission (*isnad*) of weak hadith
2. Reporting them with the exception of forged hadith
3. Following them without announcing that they are weak in all but the attributes of Allah Most High and what is possible and impossible for Him and in interpretation of His Word

Leniency is not permitted:

4. In the rules of Sacred Law like what is lawful and unlawful but is in other than that like stories, the rewards of good deeds, in admonitions and other than that
5. What is related to creed (*'aqida*) and
6. Rules of law

وَمَنْ نَقَلَ عَنْهُ ذَلِكَ ابْنُ حَنْبَلٍ وَابْنُ مَهْدِيّ وَابْنُ الْمُبَارَكِ قَالُوا إِذَا رَوَيْنَا فِي الْحَلَالِ وَالْحَرَامِ شَدَّدْنَا وَإِذَا رَوَيْنَا فِي الْفَضَائِلِ وَنَحْوِهَا تَسَاهَلْنَا .

Among those who mentioned this were [Ahmad] ibn Hanbal ﷺ and [Abd al-Rahman] ibn al-Mahdi and [Abd Allah] ibn al-Mubarak ﷺ [all of whom are outstanding authorities on hadith from the pious predecessors]. They said that when we report about the lawful and unlawful, we are strict; and when we report about the rewards of good deeds and the likes of that, we are lenient.

تَنْبِيهٌ: لَمْ يَذْكُرِ ابْنُ الصَّلَاحِ وَالْمُصَنِّفُ هُنَا وَفِي سَائِرِ كُتُبِهِ لِمَا ذَكَرَ سِوَى هَذَا الشَّرْطِ وَهُوَ كَوْنُهُ فِي الْفَضَائِلِ وَنَحْوِهَا وَذَكَرَ شَيْخُ الْإِسْلَامِ لَهُ ثَلَاثَةَ شُرُوطٍ: أَحَدُهَا أَنْ لَا يَكُونَ شَدِيد. فَيُخْرَجُ مَنِ انْفَرَدَ مِنَ الْكَذَّابِينَ وَالْمُتَّهِمِينَ بِالْكَذِبِ

وَمِنْ فُحْشِ غَلَطِهِ نَقْلَ الْعَلَائِيِّ الِاتِّفَاقَ عَلَيْهِ. الثَّانِي: أَنْ يَنْدَرِجَ تَحْتَ أَصْلٍ مَعْمُولٍ بِهِ. الثَّالِثُ: أَنْ لَا يَعْتَقِدَ عِنْدَ الْعَمَلِ بِهِ ثُبُوتَهُ بَلْ يَعْتَقِدُ الِاحْتِيَاطَ.

Notice that neither Ibn al-Salah nor the author [i.e. al-Nawawi whose work al-Suyuti is commenting on] mention here or in any other of their books any other condition save the above [for following weak hadiths]; namely, that it be in the area of the rewards of good deeds and the likes of that.[16] However, Shaykh al-Islam ⚜ [Ibn Hajar al-Asqalani] stipulated three conditions:

1. The weakness should not be severe; this condition excludes reports of liars and those suspected of lying and those who make excessive mistakes. Al-Alai declared that there is agreement on this point.
2. The report should fall under some received general precept.
3. The one who follows it should not believe positively that that hadith is confirmed; rather he is being cautious [i.e. he does what has been prescribed in the hopes of getting the reward promised].

وَقَالَ هَذَانِ ذَكَرَهُمَا ابْنُ عَبْدِ السَّلَامِ وَابْنُ دَقِيقِ الْعِيدِ وَقِيلَ لَا يَجُوزُ الْعَمَلُ بِهِ مُطْلَقًا قَالَهُ أَبُو بَكْرِ بْنُ الْعَرَبِيِّ وَقِيلَ يَعْمَلُ بِهِ مُطْلَقًا وَتَقَدَّمَ عَزْوُ ذَلِكَ إِلَى أَبِي دَاوُدَ وَأَحْمَدَ وَأَنَّهُمَا رَيَّانِ ذَلِكَ أَقْوَى مِنْ رَأْيِ الرِّجَالِ وَعِبَارَةُ الزَّرْكَشِيِّ الضَّعِيفِ مَرْدُودٌ مَا لَمْ يَقْتَضِ تَرْغِيبًا أَوْ تَرْهِيبًا أَوْ تَتَعَدَّدَ الْإِشَارَةِ وَلَمْ يَكُنِ الْمُتَابَعُ مُخْطِئًا عَنْهُ وَقِيلَ لَا يَقْبَلُ مُطْلَقًا وَقِيلَ يُقْبَلُ إِنْ شَهِدَ لَهُ أَصْلٌ وَانْدَرَجَ تَحْتَ عُمُومٍ انتهى. وَيَعْمَلُ بِالضَّعِيفِ أَيْضًا فِي الْأَحْكَامِ إِذَا كَانَ فِيهِ احْتِيَاطَ.

[Ibn Hajar] said that the [first][17] two points were stipulated by Ibn Abd al-Salam ⚜ [d. 660 / 1262; Cairo] and Ibn Daqiq al-Eid ⚜ [d. 702 / 1302; Cairo], while Abu Bakr ibn al-Arabi ⚜ [d. 543 / 1148; Fez] said that it is not permissible to follow them at all. On the other hand, some have said that it is permissible to follow them without any condition [i.e. in the area of rules of law as well as the merits of deeds for there is consensus on the other stipulation, that the hadith not be forged or suspected of it, as was mentioned above].

---

[16] Presumably, the reason they did not mention that the hadith should not be forged and that it should fall under a generally received precept of the religion as did Ibn Hajr ⚜ and others is that they took those conditions to be common knowledge and widespread. [t]
[17] The clarification that the two points referred to is the first provided by al-Sakhawi who also quoted Ibn Hajr and we will quote him presently. [t]

It was mentioned previously that this view was imputed to Abu Dawud 🙏 and Ahmad 🙏 and that the two of them maintained that weak hadith are better than the opinions of people. [Badr al-Din] al-Zarkashi 🙏 [d. 794 / 1392; Cairo] *stated it this way, "A weak hadith stands rejected unless it involves encouragement [to do good deeds] or warning [not to do bad deeds], or unless its chains of narration are more than one and the corroborating chains are not worse than the basic chain; however, it is said that it is not acceptable at all while it is also said that it will be accepted if it falls under some received precept or some general principle."*[18]

Furthermore, weak hadith are acceptable even in the rules of law if they involve precaution [in abstaining from something on account of some prohibition or warning mentioned in a weak hadith].

IMAM AL-ZARKASHI AND A PRINCIPLE AMONG SCHOLARS OF HADITH

Notice in the citation from al-Zarkashi 🙏 that he states, "*A weak hadith stand rejected unless it involves encouragement [to do good deeds] or warning [not to do bad deeds], or unless its chains of narration are more than one and the corroborating chains are not worse than the basic chain.*"

Al-Zarkashi here is evoking a received principle among the *muhaddithun* to the effect that if a weak hadith is reported with a different chain of narration then the hadith in view of the mutual corroboration will not be held weak any longer and said to be *hasan li ghairihi* or 'authentic by virtue of other than itself'. Al-Nawawi 🙏 states in his *al-Taqrib*:

$$\text{إِذَا رَأَيْتَ حَدِيثًا بِإِسْنَادٍ ضَعِيفٍ ، فَلَكَ أَنْ تَقُولَ هُوَ ضَعِيفٌ بِهَذَا الْإِسْنَادِ وَلَا}$$
$$\text{تَقُولُ ضَعِيفَ الْمَتْنِ لِمُجَرَّدِ ضَعْفِ ذَلِكَ الْإِسْنَادِ ، إِلَّا أَنْ يَقُولَ إِمَامٌ إِنَّهُ لَمْ يَرْوِ}$$
$$\text{مِنْ وَجْهٍ صَحِيحٍ أَوْ إِنَّهُ حَدِيثٌ ضَعِيفٌ مُفَسِّرٌ ضَعَفَهُ .}$$

If you see a hadith with a weak chain of narration, you are entitled to say that it is weak according to this *sanad*, but you must not say that the text [*matn*] is weak simply because that particular *sanad* is weak [because you don't know if there are other chains of narration out there corroborating this particular text], unless some Imam [who has memorized most of the corpus of hadith] declares that it hasn't been

---

[18] *Tadrib al-Rawi*, al-Suyuti, 1/298-299, Dar al-Kutub al-Ilmiyyah: Beirut, 1979. [t]

reported in any authentic form, or declares that it is weak explaining the reason for its weakness.[19]

What Imam al-Nawawi ﷺ is saying is that even if we may find a particular chain of narration to be weak, we have to refrain from dismissing the text of the hadith as weak for fear that it may be corroborated by other chains of narration, or other hadith of similar import. As al-Zarkashi has intimated in the passage we quoted above, corroboration will take place even if the other chain of narration is weak as long as it was not worse in status than the weak hadith. He meant by that, that in its chain of narration there was one suspected of lying or a confirmed liar. In further confirmation of this point consider that al-Suyuti states in his *al-Tadrib*:

وَلَا بَدْعَ فِي الْاِحْتِجَاجِ بِحَدِيثٍ لَهُ طَرِيقَانِ لَوِ انْفَرَدَ كُلٌّ مِنْهُمَا لَمْ يَكُنْ حُجَّةً، كَمَا فِي الْمُرْسَلِ، إِذَا وَرَدَ مِنْ وَجْهٍ آخَرَ مُسْنِدٍ، أَوْ وَافَقَهُ مُرْسَلٌ آخَرَ بِشَرْطِهِ كَمَا سَيَجِيءُ.

There is nothing surprising about using a hadith that has two chains of narration as a proof of the Sacred Law, even if any one of them were to exist by itself, it would not be a proof, as in the case of *mursal* [that is, the Follower reports directly from the Prophet ﷺ] for example which was reported with another chain of narration right back to the Prophet ﷺ [*musnad*], or with another *mursal* chain of narration, with a condition which we will presently mention.[20]

The condition being, as was already mentioned, that the other chain of narration not be forged. Elsewhere al-Suyuti ﷺ states:

وَكَذَا إِذَا كَانَ ضَعْفُهَا لِإِرْسَالٍ أَوْ تَدْلِيسٍ أَوْ جَهَالَةِ رِجَالٍ، كَمَا زَادَهُ شَيْخٌ، زَالَ بِمَجِيئِهِ مِنْ وَجْهٍ آخَرَ وَكَانَ دُونَ الْحَسَنِ لِذَاتِهِ.

Likewise [a weak hadith becomes strengthened to the degree of *hasan li ghairhi*] if its weakness was due to *irsal* [the Follower narrating directly from the Prophet ﷺ], or *tadlis* [when a person implies that he heard a certain Hadith from a particular Shaykh among his contemporaries][21],

---

[19] Refer to the commentary of *Tadrib al-Rawi* 296/1. [t]

[20] Transmitted from the book *Qawa'id fi 'ulum al-Hadith*, pg. 80. [t]

[21] The definition I have given in this interpolation is one type of *tadlis*; namely, what is termed *tadlis al-isnad*; for example, he says "From so-and-so." If the narrator narrates

or ignorance about a narrator [either his identity, or his status], as some authority mentioned additionally, its weakness will be removed with [the discovery] of another chain of narration, but it will not become as strong as a chain of narration that is authentic in itself.[22]

Here in this latter citation, al-Suyuti is saying that when a weak narration is corroborated it becomes *hasan*, but not as strong as what is *hasan* in its own chain of narration alone without any corroboration from another chain of narration.

Note carefully, what al-Suyuti is telling us about *mursal* narrations. In case you are not clear what a *mursal* narration is, it is a narration from a Follower, defined as one who did not see the Prophet ﷺ but saw and narrated from at least one of the Companions who ascribes directly to the Prophet ﷺ. Since a Follower by definition did not hear directly from the Prophet ﷺ, and since it is established that he is truthful, it is known that he must have narrated from at least one Companion. While the early imams including Abu Hanifah, and Malik and Ahmad, according to the famous report[23], accepted *mursal* narrations as long as its narrators were reliable and trustworthy, al-Shafi'i, and according to a report, Ahmad, and most of the *muhaddithun*, did not accept them unless they were corroborated, even if that corroboration was by means of another mursal narration.

SUMMARIZED LESSONS

To summarize what we have presented here, we can say that:

* We are encouraged to follow weakly authentic narrations in matters that involve the likes of exhortation to do good deeds or refraining from evil ones.

---

from someone with whom he was not contemporaneous, that is not deemed tadlis but rather irsal according to the famous point of view as mentioned by al-Suyuti in his *Tadrib al-Rawi* (Beirut: Dar al-Kutub al-Ilmiyah, 2nd ed., 1399/1979), 1:224. [t]

[22] Transmitted from the book *Qawa'id fi 'ulum al-Hadith*, pg. 80. [t]

[23] As mentioned in his *Tadrib al-Rawi* (Beirut: Dar al-Kutub al-Ilmiyah, 2nd ed., 1399/1979), 1:197. [t]

- We may cite such ahadith without mentioning that their chain of narration is weak, though we should not state definitely that it was something the Prophet ﷺ said, but rather that 'it has been reported that he said such-and-such'.

- We should be careful of claiming that the text of a hadith is weakly authenticated simply because the particular chain of narration that is before us is weak, for fear that it might be corroborated by another chain of narration that we are not aware of, thus misleading people incorrectly about the religion of Allah.

- We should be careful not to follow people who are hasty to write off hadith as weak although they have not memorized, or are not even familiar with, much of the corpus of hadith literature; like so many pretenders to learning in our times.

- We should bear in mind that a weakly authenticated hadith becomes strengthened to the degree of *hasan* (reliable) if it is learned that there is another chain of narration with a similar text.

Being with Allah and His Messenger ﷺ
Reflection by Habib Umar bin Hafiz [24]

THE MESSENGER OF ALLAH ﷺ said: *"A person is with the one they love."* Thus, you can gauge your love for Allah and His Messenger by gauging how much you are with them.

The Prophet ﷺ was in the highest state of being with his Lord. For that reason, he said: *"I am nothing but a slave. I eat as a slave eats and I sit as a slave sits."*

Sayyiduna Ibrahim ﷺ says in the Qur'an that it is his Lord: *"Who created me, and it is He who guides me; Who gives me food and drink."* He was always with Allah, even when he ate and drank.

One of the Knowers of Allah said: *"For twenty years people think I have been speaking to them, when in reality I have been speaking to Allah."* If you speak for His sake, in accordance with His Sacred Law and your heart is present with Him, then in reality you are speaking to Him.

The Companions and the pious people of this Umma were constantly with the Messenger of Allah ﷺ in all their states.

One of the Companions repeated three times, addressing the Prophet ﷺ: *"I love Allah and His Messenger!"* He replied ﷺ on each occasion: *"You are with the one you love."*

Sayyiduna Abu'l 'Abbas al-Mursi said: *"If the Prophet ﷺ was absent from me for an instant I would not consider myself a Muslim."*

Habib 'Umar b. 'Abd al-Rahman al-'Attas asked: *"How can he be absent from us when he is the source of our existence?"* In other words, without him, we do not exist.

---

[24] Extracts from a lesson on *Ihya 'Ulum al-Din* in Dar al-Mustafa, Tarim, on 9th Rabi al-Awwal 1436 | 31st December 2014.

Imam al-Haddad said: *"I receive from my grandfather, the Messenger of Allah, care, status, assistance, inheritance and preferential treatment."* These people reached the highest stations of being with the Beloved ﷺ.

So do not claim to love him and then depart from him. Are you with him in emulating his character? If you truly loved him, you would be with him. Do you think being with him is only in the next life? That which will be manifest in the next life is only that which is stored up in this life. If you want to be with him there, be certain that you have to be with him here.

How long have you been with your lower self (*nafs*)? It calls you to base things while Allah and His Messenger call you to lofty things. Your lower self calls you to the Fire, while they call you to Paradise. Being with Allah and His Messenger is better than being with your lower self. Your lower self is the thing which cuts you off most from being with Allah and His Messenger and it is the biggest veil between you and your Lord.

Some people reach high stations in closeness to the Beloved ﷺ before the month of Rabi is over. If you are not going to attain it in this month, then when?

When the Month of Rabi al-Awwal Arrives

Remarks by Habib Umar bin Hafiz

QUESTION

What do I do when the month of Rabi al-Awwal arrives?

ANSWER

When Rabi al-Awwal comes, open your heart to receive the divine outpouring and to attain closeness to Allah and His Beloved. Do not place anything above him. We have not been permitted to love anyone or anything, however great, as much as him. May Allah not deprive any of us of the goodness that You have because of the evil which we have.

This is the month of ennoblement—the month in which the Beloved ﷺ emerged into the world—when the blessing was completed and the earth was illuminated. Make us amongst those who receive this month in the best way.

Seek spiritual gifts through purifying your heart. Establish gatherings in every room in your house in which Allah is remembered, in which the Mawlid and Sirah are read. Do you not long for this light, for this purity, for this beauty? Are you content to turn away from it? Why exchange jewels for filth? Who tricked us into removing the speech of Allah and the Messenger and the righteous and remembrance of Allah from our houses? He informed us that the house in which the Qur'an is recited appears to those in the heavens just as the stars appear to those on the earth. This is the speech of a tongue to whose truthfulness Allah Himself testified: ﴾*He does not speak from caprice; it is no less than revelation sent down to him.*﴾ (Qur'an 53:3-4) Allah said of him: ﴾*If you obey him you will find guidance.*﴿ (Qur'an 24:54) If you want guidance in all its meanings in this life and the next, then follow My Beloved, My Chosen One.

The greatest fear is being turned away to a different direction on the day when his followers will be under his banner. On that day, it will be clear to all that the Sovereign is One, the Judge is One. Those who had been deluded in this life will be asked: ﴾*To whom belongs the Dominion today?*﴿ (Qur'an 40:16) If you do not know Muhammad ﷺ now, on that day, everyone will know him. Everyone will lower their heads to him because he is the one that Allah has chosen.

Give us sincere intentions, purify our hearts, and increase our certainty. Save the people of *la ilaha illallah*. Turn to Him—present your state to Him:

> *No created thing has any portion of this affair neither here,*
> *Nor there, so rely on the statement of the Truthful*
>
> *He is the Lord, none other, and all*
> *Are slaves under His governance without exception.*
>
> *So ask your Lord for enabling grace, forgiveness and His pleasure*
> *And to be with the people of guidance, on the path*
>
> *People that travelled to the All-Compassionate with high*
> *ambition. With truthfulness, sincerity, unobstructed*
>
> *They obtained that which is beyond all other requests*
> *By Allah what a noble and perfect life!*

—IMAM AL-HADDAD ﷺ

Dealing With Those Who Disagree With the Mawlid

Remarks by Habib Umar bin Hafiz

QUESTION

How do we deal with those who condemn
celebrating the Mawlid?

ANSWER

The Mawlid is part of the Prophetic Biography (*sirah*) and it should be treated just as the *sirah*, the remembrance of Allah and the remembrance of the Prophet ﷺ, are treated.

We should realise that the misgivings people have about the Mawlid are false and that they have been wrongly spread in the Umma. There is no valid evidence, either intellectually or in the Sacred Law, to support the prohibition of the recitation of the Mawlid. There is no text in the Sacred Law that prohibits celebrating the birth of an animal, let alone the Prophet ﷺ. Thus, reciting the Mawlid would at the very least be permissible (*mubah*). However, it is combined with acts of obedience, leads to an increase in people's faith, and increases their love for and connection to the Prophet ﷺ. It is thus regarded as being recommended (*mandub*) since it takes the ruling of the objectives that it is being used to achieve. It should be used in the best way, just as other means are used.

That being said, we must recognise that people have been affected by false beliefs. We should not be so rigid that we cause divisions amongst the Muslims and add fuel to the fire.

Some situations may dictate that the Mawlid be concealed or left out, such as when it would have a detrimental effect on the *da'wah*. It should not be left out merely in response to those who condemn it, especially when it is not expected that those people will respond to our *da'wah*. When the majority will benefit, it should not be left out.

We can also call it by another name, such as 'Commemorating the life of the Prophet' or a gathering of remembrance, knowledge, or poetry. When people find out what it contains, they will see that there is nothing in it which is impermissible.

QUESTION
Should we invite those who disagree with the Mawlid to attend?

ANSWER
Of the people that disagree with the Mawlid, some are prepared to discuss the issue and, if they can be convinced of its merit, then they can be invited to attend. If they remain unconvinced, we should show patience with them. Others may be aggressive in their rejection of the mawlid, so we should not discuss the issue with them and we should not invite them. Those who have problems with some of the things that take place in the mawlid can be invited to attend at the end of the gathering to share a meal [in love and humanity], for example.

حَوْلُ الِاحْتِفَالِ بِذِكْرِى الْمَوْلِدِ النَّبَوِيِّ الشَّرِيفِ

للسيد محمد بن علوي المالكي الحسني

بِسْمِ ٱللَّهِ ٱلرَّحْمَٰنِ ٱلرَّحِيمِ

الحمد لله رب العالمين، والصلاة والسلام على أشرف الأنبياء والمرسلين سيدنا محمد وعلى آله وصحبه وسلم .

أما بعد:

فقد كثر الكلام عن حكم الاحتفال بالمولد النبوي الشريف، وما كنت أود أن أكتب شيئاً في هذا الموضوع وذلك لأن ما شغل ذهني وذهن العقلاء من المسلمين اليوم هو أكبر من هذه القضية الجانبية التي صار الكلام عنها أشبه ما يكون بالحولية التي تُقرأ في كل موسم وتُنشر في كل عام حتى ملّ الناس سماع مثل هذا الكلام، لكن لما أحب كثير من الإخوان أن يعرفوا رأيي بالخصوص في هذا المجال، وخوفاً من أن يكون ذلك من كتم العلم أقدمت على المشاركة في الكتابة عن هذا الموضوع سائلين من المولى عَزَّ وَجَلَّ أن يلهم الجميع الصواب. آمين.

وقبل أن أسرد الأدلة على جواز الاحتفال بالمولد النبوي الشريف والاجتماع عليه أحب أن أبين المسائل الآتية.

الأولى: أننا نقول بجواز الاحتفال بالمولد النبوي الشريف والاجتماع لسماع سيرته والصلاة والسلام عليه وسماع المدائح التي تُقال في حقه، وإطعام الطعام وإدخال السرور على قلوب الأمة.

الثانية: أننا لا نقول بسنية الاحتفال بالمولد المذكور في ليلة مخصوصة بل من اعتقد ذلك فقد ابتدع في الدين، لأن ذكره ﷺ والتعلق به يجب أن يكون في كل حين، ويجب أن تمتلئ به النفوس.

نعم: إن في شهر ولادته يكون الداعي أقوى لإقبال الناس واجتماعهم وشعورهم الفياض بارتباط الزمان بعضه ببعض، فيتذكرون بالحاضر الماضي وينتقلون من الشاهد إلى الغائب.

الثالثة: أن هذه الاجتماعات هي وسيلة كبرى للدعوة إلى الله، وهي فرصة ذهبية لا تفوت، بل يجب على الدعاة والعلماء أن يذكّروا الأمة بالنبي ﷺ بأخلاقه وآدابه وأحواله وسيرته ومعاملته وعبادته، وأن ينصحوهم ويرشدوهم إلى الخير والفلاح ويحذّروهم من البلاء والبدع والشر والفتن، وإننا دائمًا ندعو إلى ذلك ونشارك في ذلك ونقول للناس:

ليس المقصود من هذه الاجتماعات مجرد الاجتماعات والمظاهر، بل هذه وسيلة شريفة إلى غاية شريفة وهي كذا وكذا، ومن لم يستفد شيئا لدينه فهو محروم من خيرات المولد الشريف.

* * *

أدلة جواز الاحتفال بمولد النبي ﷺ

الأول: أن الاحتفال بالمولد النبوي الشريف تعبير عن الفرح والسرور بالمصطفى ﷺ، وقد انتفع به الكافر.

وسيأتي في الدليل التاسع مزيد بيان لهذه المسألة، لأن أصل البرهان واحد وإن اختلفت كيفية الاستدلال وقد جرينا على هذا المنهج في هذا البحث وعليه فلا تكرار.

فقد جاء في البخاري أنه يخفف عن أبي لهب كل يوم الاثنين بسبب عتقه لثويبة جاريته لما بشّرته بولادة المصطفى ﷺ.

ويقول في ذلك الحافظ شمس الدين محمد بن ناصر الدين الدمشقي:

إِذَا كَانَ هَذَا كَافِرًا جَاءَ ذَمُّهُ بِتَبَّتْ يَدَاهُ فِي الْجَحِيمِ مُخَلَّدًا
أَتَى أَنَّهُ فِي يَوْمِ الْإِثْنَيْنِ دَائِمًا يُخَفَّفُ عَنْهُ لِلسُّرُورِ بِأَحْمَدَا
فَمَا الظَّنُّ بِالْعَبْدِ الَّذِي عُمْرُهُ كَانَ بِأَحْمَدَ مَسْرُورًا وَمَاتَ مُوَحِّدًا

وهذه القصة رواها البخاري في الصحيح في كتاب النكاح مرسلة ونقلها الحافظ ابن حجر في الفتح ورواها الإمام عبدالرزاق الصنعاني في المصنف والحافظ البيهقي في الدلائل وابن كثير في السيرة النبوية من البداية ومحمد ابن عمر بحرق في حدائق الأنوار والحافظ البغوي في شرح السنة وابن هشام والسهيلي في الروض الأُنُف والعامري في بهجة المحافل،

وهي وإنْ كانت مرسلة إلا أنها مقبولة لأجل نقل البخاري لها واعتماد العلماء من الحفاظ لذلك ولكونها في المناقب والخصائص لا في الحلال والحرام، وطلاب العلم يعرفون الفرق في الاستدلال بالحديث بين المناقب والأحكام، وأما انتفاع الكفار بأعمالهم ففيه كلام بين العلماء ليس هذا محل بسطه، والأصل فيه ما جاء في الصحيح من التخفيف عن أبي طالب بطلب من الرسول ﷺ.

الثاني: أنه ﷺ كان يعظّم يوم مولده، ويشكر الله تعالى فيه على نعمته الكبرى عليه، وتفضّله عليه بالجود لهذا الوجود، إذ سعد به كل موجود، وكان يعبّر عن ذلك التعظيم بالصيام كما جاء في الحديث عن أبي قتادة:

أن رسول الله ﷺ سُئل عن صيام يوم الاثنين؟ فقال (فيه وُلدتُ وفيه أُنزل عليّ) رواه الإمام مسلم في الصحيح في كتاب الصيام.

وهذا في معنى الاحتفال به، إلّا أن الصورة مختلفة ولكن المعنى موجود سواء كان ذلك بصيام أو إطعام طعام أو اجتماع على ذكر أو صلاة على النبي ﷺ أو سماع شمائله الشريفة.

الثالث: أن الفرح به ﷺ مطلوب بأمر القرآن من قوله تعالى (قل بفضل الله وبرحمته فبذلك فليفرحوا) فالله تعالى أمرنا أن نفرح بالرحمة، والنبي ﷺ أعظم الرحمة، قال الله تعالى (وما أرسلناك إلا رحمة للعالمين).

الرابع: أن النبي ﷺ كان يلاحظ ارتباط الزمان بالحوادث الدينية العظمى التي مضت وانقضت، فإذا جاء الزمان الذي وقعت فيه كان فرصة لتذكّرها وتعظيم يومها لأجلها ولأنه ظرف لها.

وقد أصّل ﷺ هذه القاعدة بنفسه كما صرح في الحديث الصحيح أنه ﷺ: لما وصل المدينة ورأى اليهود يصومون يوم عاشوراء سأل عن ذلك فقيل له: إنهم يصومون لأن الله نجّى نبيهم وأغرق عدوهم فهم يصومونه شكرا لله على هذه النعمة، فقال ﷺ: نحن أولى بموسى منكم، فصامه وأمر بصيامه.

الخامس: أن المولد الشريف يبعث على الصلاة والسلام المطلوبين بقوله تعالى: ﴿إن الله وملائكته يصلّون على النبي يا أيها الذين آمنوا صلّوا عليه وسلّموا تسليما﴾.

وما كان يبعث على المطلوب شرعاً فهو مطلوب شرعاً، فكم للصلاة عليه من فوائد نبوية، وإمدادات محمدية، يسجد القلم في محراب البيان عاجزاً عن تعداد آثارها ومظاهر أنوارها.

السادس: أن المولد الشريف يشتمل على ذكر مولده الشريف ومعجزاته وسيرته والتعريف به، أولسنا مأمورين بمعرفته ومطالبين بالاقتداء به والتأسّي بأعماله والإيمان بمعجزاته والتصديق بآياته؟ وكتب المولد تؤدي هذا المعنى تماما.

السابع: التعرّض لمكافأته بأداء بعض ما يجب له علينا ببيان أوصافه الكاملة وأخلاقه الفاضلة، وقد كان الشعراء يفدون إليه ﷺ بالقصائد ويرضى عملهم، ويجزيهم على ذلك بالطيبات والصلات، فإذا كان يرضى عمن مدحه فكيف لا يرضى عمن جمع شمائله الشريفة، ففي ذلك التقرب له ﷺ باستجلاب محبته ورضاه.

الثامن: أن معرفة شمائله ومعجزاته وإرهاصاته تستدعي كمال الإيمان به ﷺ، وزيادة المحبة، إذ الإنسان مطبوع على حب الجميل، ولا أجمل ولا أكمل ولا أفضل من أخلاقه وشمائله ﷺ، وزيادة المحبة وكمال الإيمان مطلوبان شرعاً، فما

كان يستدعيهما فهو مطلوب كذلك.

التاسع: أن تعظيمه ﷺ مشروع، والفرح بيوم ميلاده الشريف بإظهار السرور وصنع الولائم والاجتماع للذكر وإكرام الفقراء من أظهر مظاهر التعظيم والابتهاج والفرح والشكر لله بما هدانا لدينه القويم وما منَّ به علينا من بعثه عليه أفضل الصلاة والتسليم.

العاشر: يؤخذ من قوله ﷺ في فضل يوم الجمعة وعدِّ مزاياه: (وفيه خُلق آدم) تشريف الزمان الذي ثبت أنه ميلاد لأي نبيّ كان من الأنبياء عليهم السلام، فكيف باليوم الذي وُلد فيه أفضل النبيين وأشرف المرسلين.

ولا يختص هذا التعظيم بذلك اليوم بعينه بل يكون له خصوصاً، ولنوعه عموماً مهما تكرر كما هو الحال في يوم الجمعة شُكراً للنعمة وإظهاراً لمزية النبوة وإحياءً للحوادث التاريخية الخطيرة ذات الإصلاح المهم في تاريخ الإنسانية وجبهة الدهر وصحيفة الخلود، كما يؤخذ تعظيم المكان الذي وُلد فيه نبيٌّ من أمر جبريل عليه السلام النبيَّ ﷺ بصلاة ركعتين ببيت لحم، ثم قال له: (أتدري أين صلّيت ؟ قال: لا، قال: صلّيتَ ببيت لحم حيث وُلد عيسى) كما جاء ذلك في حديث شداد بن أوس الذي رواه البزّار وأبو يعلى والطبراني. قال الحافظ الهيثمي في مجمع الزوائد: ورجاله رجال الصحيح، وقد نقل هذه الرواية الحافظ ابن حجر في الفتح وسكت عنها.

الحادي عشر: أن المولد أمرٌ استحسنه العلماء والمسلمون في جميع البلاد، وجرى به العمل في كل صقع فهو مطلوب شرعاً للقاعدة المأخوذة من حديث ابن مسعود

رَضِيَ اللهُ عَنْهُ الموقوف (ما رآه المسلمون حسناً فهو عند الله حسن، وما رآه المسلمون قبيحاً فهو عند الله قبيح) أخرجه أحمد.

الثاني عشر : أن المولد اشتمل على اجتماع وذكر وصدقة ومدح وتعظيم للجناب النبوي فهو سنة، وهذه أمور مطلوبة شرعاً وممدوحة وجاءت الآثار الصحيحة بها وبالحثّ عليها.

الثالث عشر : أن الله تعالى قال : (وكلاً نقصُّ عليك من أنباء الرسل ما نثبّت به فؤادك) فهذا يظهر منه أن الحكمة في قصّ أنباء الرسل عليهم السلام تثبيت فؤاده الشريف بذلك ولا شك أننا اليوم نحتاج إلى تثبيت أفئدتنا بأنبائه وأخباره أشد من احتياجه هو ﷺ.

الرابع عشر : ليس كل ما لم يفعله السلف ولم يكن في الصدر الأول فهو بدعة منكرة سيئة يحرم فعلها ويجب الإنكار عليها بل يجب أن يعرض ما أحدث على أدلة الشرع فما اشتمل على مصلحة فهو واجب، أو على محرّم فهو محرّم، أو على مكروه فهو مكروه، أو على مباح فهو مباح، أو على مندوب فهو مندوب، وللوسائل حكم المقاصد،

ثم قسّم العلماء البدعة إلى خمسة أقسام:

واجبة:

كالرد على أهل الزيغ وتعلّم النحو.

ومندوبة:

كإحداث الربط والمدارس، والأذان على المنائر وصنع إحسان لم يعهد في الصدر الأول.

ومكروه:

كزخرفة المساجد وتزويق المصاحف.

ومباحة:

كاستعمال المنخل، والتوسع في المأكل والمشرب.

ومحرمة:

وهي ما أحدث لمخالفة السنة ولم تشمله أدلة الشرع العامة ولم يحتو على مصلحة شرعية

الخامس عشر: فليست كل بدعة محرّمة، ولو كان كذلك لحرُم جمع أبي بكر وعمر وزيد رضي الله عنهم القرآن وكتبه في المصاحف خوفاً على ضياعه بموت الصحابة القراء رضي الله عنهم، ولحرم جمع عمر رضي الله عنه الناس على إمام واحد في صلاة القيام مع قوله (نعمت البدعة هذه) وحرم التصنيف في جميع العلوم النافعة ولوجب علينا حرب الكفار بالسهام والأقواس مع حربهم لنا بالرصاص والمدافع والدبابات والطيارات والغواصات والأساطيل، وحرم الأذان على المنائر واتخاذ الربط والمدارس والمستشفيات والإسعاف ودار اليتامى والسجون،

فمن ثَمَّ قيّد العلماء رضي الله عنهم حديث (كل بدعة ضلالة) بالبدعة السيئة، ويصرّح بهذا القيد ما وقع من أكبر الصحابة والتابعين من المحدثات التي لم تكن في زمنه ﷺ، ونحن اليوم قد أحدثنا مسائل كثيرة لم يفعلها السلف وذلك كجمع الناس على إمام واحد في آخر الليل لأداء صلاة التهجد بعد صلاة التراويح، وكختم المصحف فيها وكقراءة دعاء ختم القرآن وكخطبة الإمام ليلة سبع وعشرين في صلاة التهجد وكنداء المنادي بقوله (صلاة القيام أثابكم الله) فكل هذا لم يفعله النبي ﷺ ولا أحد من السلف فهل يكون فعلنا له بدعة؟

السادس عشر: فالاحتفال بالمولد وإن لم يكن في عهده ﷺ فهو بدعة، ولكنها حسنة لاندراجها تحت الأدلة الشرعية، والقواعد الكلية، فهي بدعة باعتبار هيئتها الاجتماعية لا باعتبار أفرادها لوجود أفرادها في العهد النبوي عُلم ذلك في الدليل الثاني عشر.

السابع عشر: وكل ما لم يكن في الصدر الأول بهيئته الاجتماعية لكن أفراده موجودة يكون مطلوباً شرعاً، لأن ما ترّكب من المشروع فهو مشروع كما لا يخفى.

الثامن عشر: قال الإمام الشافعي رَضِيَاللهُعَنهُ: ما أحدث وخالف كتاباً أو سنة أو إجماعاً أو أثراً فهو البدعة الضالة، وما أحدث من الخير ولم يخالف شيئاً من ذلك فهو المحمود. ا. هـ.

وجرى الإمام العز بن عبد السلام والنووي كذلك وابن الأثير على تقسيم البدعة إلى ما أشرنا إليه سابقاً.

التاسع عشر: فكل خير تشمله الأدلة الشرعية ولم يقصد بإحداثه مخالفة الشريعة ولم يشتمل على منكر فهو من الدين.

وقول المتعصب إن هذا لم يفعله السلف ليس هو دليلاً له بل هو عدم دليل كما لا يخفى على مَن مارس علم الأصول، فقد سمى الشارع بدعة الهدى سنة ودفاعها وعدَّ فاعلها أجراً فقال عَلَيهِالسَّلَامُوَالصَّلَاة: (مَن سنَّ في الإسلام سنة حسنة فعمل بها بعده كُتب له أجر مَن عمل بها ولا ينقص من أجورهم شيء).

العشرون: أن الاحتفال بالمولد النبوي إحياء لذكرى المصطفى ﷺ وذلك مشروع عندنا في الإسلام، فأنت ترى أن أكثر أعمال الحج إنما هي إحياء لذكريات مشهودة ومواقف محمودة فالسعي بين الصفا والمروة ورمي الجمار والذبح بمنى كلها حوادث ماضية سابقة، يحيي المسلمون ذكراها بتجديد صُورِها في الواقع والدليل على ذلك قوله تعالى: (وأذِّن في الناس بالحج) وقوله تعالى حكاية عن إبراهيم وإسماعيل عليهما السلام (وأرنا مناسكنا).

الحادي والعشرون: كل ما ذكرناه سابقا من الوجوه في مشروعية المولد إنما هو في المولد الذي خلا من المنكرات المذمومة التي يجب الإنكار عليها، أما إذا اشتمل

المولد على شئ ما يجب الإنكار عليه كاختلاط الرجال بالنساء وارتكاب المحرمات وكثرة الإسراف ما لا يرضى به صاحب المولد ﷺ فهذا الاشك في تحريمه ومنعه لما اشتمل عليه من المحرمات لكن تحريمه حينئذ يكون عارضاً لا ذاتياً كما لا يخفى على مَن تأمّل ذلك.

* * *

رأي الشيخ ابن تيمية في المولد

يقول: قد يُثاب بعض الناس على فعل المولد، وكذلك ما يحدثه بعض الناس إما مضاهاة للنصارى في ميلاد عيسى ﷺ وإما محبة للنبي ﷺ وتعظيماً له، والله قد يثيبهم على هذه المحبة والاجتهاد لا على البدع.

ثم قال: واعلم أن من الأعمال ما يكون فيه خير لاشتماله على أنواع من المشروع، وفيه أيضاً شر من بدعة وغيرها فيكون ذلك العمل شراً بالنسبة إلى الإعراض عن الدين بالكلية كحال المنافقين والفاسقين.

وهذا قد ابتلي به أكثر الأمة في الأزمان المتأخرة، فعليك هنا بأدبين.

أحدهما: أن يكون حرصك على التمسك بالسنة باطناً وظاهراً في خاصتك وخاصة من يطيعك واعرف المعروف وأنكر المنكر.

الثاني: أن تدعو الناس إلى السنة بحسب الإمكان، فإذا رأيت من يعمل هذا ولا يتركه إلا إلى شر منه فلا تَدْعُ إلى ترك المنكر بفعل ما هو أنكر منه أو بترك واجب أو مندوب تركه أضر من فعل ذلك المكروه، ولكن إذا كان في البدعة نوع من الخير فعوّض عنه من الخير المشروع بحسب المكان، إذ النفوس لا تترك شيئاً إلا بشيء ولا ينبغي لأحد أن يترك خيراً إلا إلى مثله أو إلى خير منه.

ثم قال: فتعظيم المولد واتخاذه موسماً قد يفعله بعض الناس ويكون له فيه أجر عظيم لحسن قصده وتعظيمه لرسول الله ﷺ كما قدمته لك أنه يحسن من بعض الناس ما يستقبح من المؤمن المسدد، ولهذا قيل للإمام أحمد عن بعض الأمراء

إنه أنفق على مصحف ألف دينار ونحو ذلك فقال: دعه فهذا أفضل ما أنفق فيه الذهب، أو كما قال، مع أن مذهبه: أن زخرفة المصاحف مكروهة، وقد تأول بعض الأصحاب أنه أنفقها في تجديد الورق والخط، وليس مقصود الإمام أحمد هذا وإنما قصده أن هذا العمل فيه مصلحة وفيه أيضاً مفسدة كُره لأجلها

★   ★   ★

مفهوم المولد في نظري

إننا نرى أن الاحتفال بالمولد النبوي الشريف ليست له كيفية مخصوصة لابد من الالتزام أو إلزام الناس بها، بل إن كل ما يدعو إلى الخير ويجمع الناس على الهدى ويرشدهم إلى ما فيه منفعتهم في دينهم ودنياهم يحصل به تحقيق المقصود من المولد النبوي.

ولذلك فلو اجتمعنا على شئ من المدائح التي فيها ذكر الحبيب ﷺ وفضله وجهاده وخصائصه ولم نقرأ القصة التي تعارف الناس على قراءتها واصطلحوا عليها حتى ظن البعض أن المولد النبوي لا يتم إلا بها، ثم استمعنا إلى ما يلقيه المتحدثون من مواعظ وإرشادات وإلى ما يتلوه القارئ من آيات.

أقول: لو فعلنا ذلك فإن ذلك داخل تحت المولد النبوي الشريف ويتحقق به معنى الاحتفال بالمولد النبوي الشريف، وأظن أن هذا المعنى لا يختلف عليه اثنان ولا ينتطح فيه عنزان.

★ ★ ★

القيام في المولد

أما القيام في المولد النبوي عند ذكر ولادته ﷺ وخروجه إلى الدنيا، فإن بعض الناس يظن ظناً باطلاً لا أصل له عند أهل العلم فيما أعلم بل عند أجهل الناس ممن يحضر المولد ويقوم مع القائمين، وذاك الظن السيء هو أن الناس يقومون معتقدين أن النبي ﷺ يدخل إلى المجلس في تلك اللحظة بجسده الشريف، ويزيد سوء الظن ببعضهم فيرى أن البخور والطيب له وأن الماء الذي يوضع في وسط المجلس ليشرب منه.

وكل هذه الظنون لا تخطر ببال عاقل من المسلمين، وإننا نبرأ إلى الله من كل ذلك لما في ذلك من الجراءة على مقام رسول الله ﷺ والحكم على جسده الشريف بما لا يعتقده إلا ملحد مفتر وأمور البرزخ لا يعلمها إلا الله ﷻ.

والنبي ﷺ أعلى من ذلك وأكمل وأجل من أن يُقال في حقه إنه يخرج من قبره ويحضر بجسده في مجلس كذا في ساعة كذا أقول: هذا افتراء محض وفيه من الجراءة والوقاحة والقباحة ما لا يصدر إلا من مبغض حاقد أو جاهل معاند.

نعم إننا نعتقد أنه ﷺ حيٌّ حياة برزخية كاملة لائقة بمقامه، ومقتضى تلك الحياة الكاملة العليا تكون روحه ﷺ جوّالة سيّاحة في ملكوت الله ﷻ ويمكن أن تحضر مجالس الخير ومشاهد النور والعلم، وكذلك أرواح خُلّص المؤمنين من أتباعه، وقد قال الإمام مالك: بلغني أن الروح مرسلة تذهب حيث شاءت.

وقال سلمان الفارسي: أرواح المؤمنين في برزخ من الأرض تذهب حيث شاءت (كذا في الروح لابن القيم).

إذا علمت هذا فاعلم أن القيام في المولد النبوي ليس بواجب ولا سنة ولا يصح اعتقاد ذلك أبداً، وإنما هي حركة يعبّر بها الناس عن فرحهم وسرورهم فإذا ذكر أنه ﷺ ولد وخرج إلى الدنيا يتصور السامع في تلك اللحظة أن الكون كله يهتز فرحاً وسروراً بهذه النعمة فيقوم مظهراً لذلك الفرح والسرور معبّراً عنه، فهي مسألة عادية محضة لادينية، إنها ليست عبادة ولا شريعة ولا سنة وما هي إلا أنْ جرت عادة الناس بها.

* * *

استحسان العلماء لقيام المولد وبيان وجوهه

واستحسن ذلك من استحسنه من أهل العلم، وقد أشار إلى ذلك البرزنجي مؤلف أحد الموالد بنفسه إذ قال بالنّص: (وقد استحسن القيام عند ذكر مولده الشريف أئمةٌ ذوو رواية ورويّه، فطوبى لمن كان تعظيمه ﷺ غاية مرامه ومرماه)، ونعني بالاستحسان للشئ هنا كونه جائزاً من حيث ذاته وأصله ومحموداً مطلوباً من حيث بواعثه وعواقبه، لا بالمعنى المصطلح عليه في أصول الفقه، وأقل الطلاب علماً يعرف أن كلمة (استحسن) يجري استعمالها في الأمور العادية المتعارف عليها بين الناس فيقولون: استحسنت هذا الكتاب وهذا الأمر مستحسن واستحسن الناس هذه الطريقة، ومرادهم بذلك كله هو الاستحسان العادي اللغوي وإلا كانت أمور الناس أصولاً شرعية ولا يقول بهذا عاقل أو مَن عنده أدنى إلمام بالأصول.

*   *   *

وجوه استحسان القيام

الوجه الأول: أنه جرى عليه العمل في سائر الأقطار والأمصار واستحسنه العلماء شرقاً وغرباً، والقصد به تعظيم صاحب المولد الشريف ﷺ، وما استحسنه المسلمون فهو عند الله حسن، وما استقبحوه فهو عند الله قبيح كما تقدم في الحديث.

الوجه الثاني: أن القيام لأهل الفضل مشروع ثابت بالأدلة الكثيرة من السنة، وقد ألف الإمام النووي في ذلك جزءاً مستقلاً وأيده ابن حجر وردّ على ابن الحاج الذي ردّ عليه بجزء آخر سماه رفع الملام عن القائل باستحسان القيام.

الوجه الثالث: ورد في الحديث المتفق عليه قوله ﷺ للأنصار (قوموا إلى سيدكم) وهذا القيام كان تعظيماً لسيدنا سعد رضي الله عنه ولم يكن من أجل كونه مريضاً وإلا لقال قوموا إلى مريضكم ولم يقل إلى سيدكم ولم يأمر الجميع بالقيام بل كان قد أمر البعض.

الوجه الرابع: كان من هدي النبي ﷺ أن يقوم تعظيماً للداخل عليه وتأليفاً كما قام لابنته السيدة فاطمة وأقرها على تعظيمها له بذلك، وأمر الأنصار بقيامهم لسيدهم فدلّ ذلك على مشروعية القيام، ﷺ أحق من عظّم لذلك.

الوجه الخامس: قد يقال إن ذلك في حياته وحضوره ﷺ، وهو في حالة المولد غير حاضر ﷺ، فالجواب عن ذلك أن قارئ المولد الشريف مستحضر له بتشخيص ذاته الشريفة، وهذا التصور شئ محمود ومطلوب بل لابد أن يتوفر في ذهن المسلم الصادق في كل حين ليكمل اتباعه له ﷺ وتزيد محبته فيه ويكون هواه تبعاً لما جاء به.

فالناس يقومون احتراماً وتقديراً لهذا التصور الواقع في نفوسهم عن شخصية ذلك الرسول العظيم مستشعرين جلال الموقف وعظمة المقام وهو أمر عادي -كما تقدم- ويكون استحضار الذاكر ذلك موجباً لزيادة تعظيمه ﷺ.

* * *

الكتب المصنفة في هذا الباب

الكتب المصنفة في هذا الباب كثيرة جداً، منها المنظوم ومنها المنثور ومنها المختصر والمطول والوسط، ولا نزيد في هذه العجالة الموجزة أن نستوعب ذكر ذلك كله لكثرته وسعته، وكذلك لا نستطيع أن نقتصر على ذكر شئ من ذلك على وجه الإجمال، لأنه ليس مصنف أولى من مصنف في تقديم ذكره، وإن كان لابد أن يكون بعضها أفضل وأجلّ من بعض، ولذلك فإني سأقتصر هنا على ذكر كبار علماء الأمة من الحفّاظ الأئمة الذين صنّفوا في هذا الباب وظهرت لهم موالد مشهورة معروفة.

فمنهم الحافظ محمد بن أبي بكر بن عبد الله القيسي الدمشقي الشافعي المعروف بالحافظ ابن ناصر الدين الدمشقي المولود سنة (٧٧٧ هـ) والمتوفَّى سنة (٨٤٢ هـ) قال عنه الحافظ ابن فهد في لحظ الألحاظ ذيل تذكرة الحفاظ صفحة ٣١٩: هو إمام حافظ مفيد مؤرخ مجيد له الذهن الصافي السالم الصحيح والخط الجيد المليح على طريقة أهل الحديث، وقال: كتب الكثير وعلّق وحشّى وأثبت وطبق وبرز على أقرانه وتقدم وأفاد كل مَن إليه يمّم.

وقد تولّى مشيخة دار الحديث الأشرفية بدمشق، وقال عنه الإمام السيوطي: صار محدّث البلاد الدمشقية، وقال الشيخ محمد زاهد في تعليقه على ذيل الطبقات: قال الحافظ جمال الدين بن عبدالهادي الحنبلي في الرياض اليانعة لما ترجم لابن ناصر الدين المذكور: كان معظِّماً للشيخ ابن تيمية محباً له مبالغاً في محبته .ا.هـ. قلت: وقد ذكر له ابن فهد مؤلفاً يُسمى (الرد الوافر على مَن زعم أن من سمى ابن تيمية شيخ الاسلام كافر) قلت: هذا الإمام قد صنف في المولد الشريف أجزاء عديدة،

فمن ذلك ما ذكره صاحب كشف الظنون عن أسامي الكتب والفنون صفحة ٣١٩ وجامع الآثار في مولد النبي المختار في ثلاث مجلدات واللفظ الرائق في مولد خير الخلائق وهو مختصر .ا.هـ. وقال ابن فهد وله أيضاً مورد الصادي في مولد الهادي. ومن أولئك الحافظ عبدالرحيم بن الحسين بن عبدالرحمن المصري الشهير بالحافظ العراقي المولود سنة ٧٢٥ هـ والمتوفَّى سنة ٨٠٨ هـ.

وهو الإمام الكبير الشهير أبو الفضل زين الدين وحيد عصره وفريد دهره حافظ الإسلام وعمدة الأنام العلّامة الحجة الحبر الناقد مَن فاق بالحفظ والاتقان في زمانه وشهد له بالتفرد في فنه أئمة عصره وأوانه، برع في الحديث والإسناد والحفظ والإتقان، وصار المشار إليه في الديار المصرية بالمعرفة، وماذا أقول في إمام كهذا وبحر خضم وفحل من فحول السنة وطود عظيم من أركان هذا الدين الحنيف، ويكفينا قبول الناس لقوله في الحديث والإسناد والمصطلح ورجوعهم إليه إذا قيل العراقي، وألفيته في هذا الباب عليها الاعتماد ويعرفه فضلاً وعلماً كل مَن له أدنى معرفة وصِلة بالحديث، إن هذا الإمام قد صنّف مولداً شريفاً أسماه (المورد الهني في المولد السني) ذكره ضمن مؤلفاته غير واحد من الحفاظ مثل ابن فهد والسيوطي في ذيولهما على التذكرة.

ومن أولئك الحافظ محمد بن عبدالرحمن بن محمد القاهري المعروف بالحافظ السخاوي المولود سنة ٨٣١هـ والمتوفَّى سنة ٩٠٢هـ بالمدينة المنورة، وهو المؤرخ الكبير والحافظ الشهير ترجمه الإمام الشوكاني في البدر الطالع وقال: هو من الأئمة الأكابر، وقال ابن فهد: لم أرَ في الحفاظ المتأخرين مثله، وهوله اليد الطولى في المعرفة وأسماء الرجال وأحوال الرواة والجرح والتعديل

وإليه يُشار في ذلك، حتى قال بعض العلماء: لم يأتِ بعد الحافظ الذهبي مثله سلك هذا المسلك وبعده مات فن الحديث، وقال الشوكاني: ولو لم يكن له من التصنيف إلا الضوء اللامع لكان أعظم دليل على إمامته، قلت: وقد قال في كشف الظنون: إن للحافظ السخاوي جزءاً في المولد الشريف ﷺ.

ومن أولئك الحافظ المجتهد الإمام ملا علي قاري بن سلطان بن محمد الهروي المتوفى سنة ١٠١٤هـ صاحب شرح المشكاة وغيرها. ترجمه الشوكاني في البدر الطالع وقال: قال العصامي في وصفه هو الجامع للعلوم النقلية والمتضلّع من السنة النبوية أحد جماهير الأعلام ومشاهير أولي الحفظ والأفهام، ثم قال: لكنه امتحن بالاعتراض على الأئمة لاسيما الشافعي ا.هـ. ثم تكلف الشوكاني وقام يدافع وينافح عن ملا علي قاري بعد سوقه كلام العصامي، فقال: أقول هذا دليل على علو منزلته فإن المجتهد شأنه أن يبين ما يخالف الأدلة الصحيحة ويعترضه سواء كان قائله عظيماً أو حقيراً، تلك شكاة ظاهر عنك عارها.

قلت: هذا الإمام المجتهد المحدّث ترجم له الشوكاني الذي قالوا عنه إنه مجتهد ومحدّث قد صنّف في مولد الرسول ﷺ كتاباً قال صاحب كشف الظنون: واسمه (المورد الروي في المولد النبوي) قلت: وقد حقّقتُهُ بفضل الله وعلّقتُ عليه وطبعته لأول مرة. ومن أولئك الحافظ عماد الدين إسماعيل بن عمر بن كثير صاحب التفسير.

قال الذهبي في المختص: الإمام المفتي المحدّث البارع ثقة متفنن محدّث متقن ا.هـ. وترجمه الشهاب احمد بن حجر العسقلاني في الدرر الكامنة في أعيان المائة الثامنة في صفحة ٣٧٤ جاء منها: أنه اشتغل بالحديث مطالعة في متونه ورجاله،

وقال: وأخذ عن ابن تيمية ففتن بحبه وامتحن لسببه، وكان كثير الاستحضار حسن المفاكهة، سار تصانيفه في البلاد في حياته وانتفع بها الناس بعد وفاته سنة ٧٤٤هـ وقد صنّف الإمام ابن كثير مولداً نبوياً طُبع أخيراً بتحقيق الدكتور صلاح الدين المنجد.

ومن أولئك الحافظ وجيه الدين عبدالرحمن بن علي بن محمد الشيباني اليمني الزبيدي الشافعي (المعروف بابن الديبع ، والديبع بمعنى الأبيض بلغة السودان هو لقب لجده الأعلى علي بن يوسف) ولد في المحرم سنة ٨٦٦هـ وتوفي يوم الجمعة ثاني عشر من رجب الفرد سنة ٩٤٤هـ وكان رحمه الله أحد أئمة الزمان، إليه انتهت مشيخة الحديث، حدّث بالبخاري أكثر من مائة مرة وقرأه مرة في ستة أيام. وقد صنّف مولداً نبوياً مشهوراً في كثير من البلاد وقد حققناه وعلّقنا عليه وخرّجنا أحاديثه بفضل الله.

وكتبه

محمد علوي المالكي الحسني

خادم العلم الشريف ببلد الله الحرام

م

Made in the USA
Middletown, DE
08 February 2025

70606412R00060